HOTEL PALACE LUZERN
DENKMALPFLEGERISCHE
ERNEUERUNG

HOTEL PALACE LUCERNE
HERITAGE RENOVATION

HOTEL PALACE LUZERN
DENKMALPFLEGERISCHE
ERNEUERUNG

HOTEL PALACE LUCERNE
HERITAGE RENOVATION

PALACE

IWAN BÜHLER
ARCHITEKTEN

QUART

VORWORT

Kuno Zimmermann & Franziska Willers
Itten+Brechbühl AG, Zürich

Die Itten+Brechbühl AG wurde von der Bauherrschaft, der Han's Holdings Group Ltd., mit der Gesamtleitung und dem Baumanagement der Sanierung des Hotel Palace in Luzern beauftragt. Wir bedanken uns bei der Bauherrschaft für das grosse entgegengebrachte Vertrauen und das Mandat herzlichst. Der Bauherrschaft und dem Betreiber, der Mandarin Oriental Hotel Group, gratulieren wir zu diesem einmaligen Bauwerk und wir sind stolz darauf, Teil des Teams für dieses anspruchsvolle Projekt gewesen zu sein.

Die Gesamtsanierung eines denkmalgeschützten und historisch hervorstechenden Gebäudes zu koordinieren und zu realisieren, ist äusserst anspruchsvoll und manchmal auch ein bisschen abenteuerlich. Gerade bei einem Gebäude wie dem Hotel Palace in Luzern, welches in seiner 120-jährigen Geschichte schon mehrmals saniert, erneuert und umgebaut wurde, betritt man unbekanntes Terrain. Hinter jeder Wand und unter jedem Bodenbelag kann sich eine Überraschung verbergen, auf die spontan reagiert werden muss.

Komplett wird das Abenteuer, wenn weitere Herausforderungen auf das Bauprojekt treffen, wie beispielsweise der Eintritt des Betreibers während der fortgeschrittenen Planungs- und Bauarbeiten, eine Pandemie mit schweren und noch nie dagewesenen Einschränkungen und die daraus resultierenden Lieferverzügen.

Nicht zuletzt erfordert das Zusammenspiel aus einer internationalen Bauherrschaft mit dem ebenfalls internationalen Hotelbetreiber sowie Planern und Planerinnen und Handwerkern und Handwerkerinnen aus verschiedenen Ländern ein grosses Fingerspitzengefühl in der Orchestrierung.

Nach gut vier Jahren Abenteuerreise haben wir gemeinsam die gesteckten Ziele glanzvoll erreicht und dürfen uns über ein wunderschön renoviertes Hotel der Luxusklasse in bester Lage am Vierwaldstättersee freuen. Als Teil des Gesamtleitungsteams konnten wir den Puls dieses Projekts hautnah steuern und miterleben. Dabei durften wir nicht nur die Fäden ziehen, sondern oft auch zwischen verschiedenen Kulturen, Ländern, Sprachen und Zielvorstellungen vermitteln.

FOREWORD

Kuno Zimmermann & Franziska Willers
Itten+Brechbühl AG, Zurich

Itten+Brechbühl AG was contracted by the client, Han's Holdings Group Ltd, to assume overall project responsibility and take over the building management for the refurbishment of the Hotel Palace in Lucerne. We wish to thank the client for the great trust it invested in us and for its mandate. Congratulations to the client and the hotel operator, the Mandarin Oriental Hotel Group, on this unique building. We are proud to have been part of the team that implemented this ambitious project.

Coordinating and implementing the overall renovation of a preservation-listed, historically prominent building is extremely demanding and sometimes rather adventurous. It involves entering unknown territory, especially in the case of a building like the Hotel Palace in Lucerne, which has been refurbished, renovated and converted several times during its 120-year history. A surprise may be hidden behind each wall and beneath each floor, demanding a spontaneous reaction.

The adventure is complete when the building project faces several challenges at once, such as the hotel operator's introduction during advanced planning and construction work, a pandemic entailing serious and unprecedented limitations, as well as the resulting supply constraints.

Coordinating between the international client, the international hotel operator, and planners and trades from various countries is a delicate process requiring a sense of tact in orchestrating the measures.

After over four years on our adventure together, we have shined in achieving our defined goals and can enjoy the magnificent, renovated luxury hotel at its marvellous location by Lake Lucerne. As part of the overall management team, we were able to steer the project from its heart and experience it at close proximity. In doing so, we were not only able to pull the strings, but also mediate between various cultures, countries, languages and envisaged goals. Thanks to the efforts of all participants and despite all of these challenges, we have managed to implement an impressive project that will please locals and international guests alike. All the project participants can be proud of having dared to implement the project and mastered every stage with great commitment, considerable flexibility and close collaboration. I hope this book demonstrates

Dank dem Effort aller Beteiligten haben wir es geschafft, trotz all dieser Herausforderungen ein Projekt umzusetzen, das überzeugt und der lokalen und internationalen Gästeschar Freude machen wird. Alle Projektbeteiligten dürfen stolz sein, dieses Vorhaben gewagt und alle Schritte mit grossem Einsatz sowie viel Flexibilität und in enger Zusammenarbeit gemeistert zu haben. Ich hoffe, wir können für Sie mit diesem Buch die grosse Arbeit, die hinter der Sanierung steckt, sichtbar machen.

Wir wünschen Ihnen viel Freude bei der Lektüre und natürlich viel Genuss und Erholung bei einer Übernachtung in einem der 136 neu gestalteten Zimmer des Mandarin Oriental Palace in Luzern.

the amount of work that lies behind the refurbishing measures.

We also hope you enjoy reading this volume and naturally invite you to visit and relax in one of the 136 newly designed rooms at the Mandarin Oriental Palace in Lucerne.

NEUBAU 1906
NEW BUILDING IN 1906

**Seiten 8–21: Aussen- und Innenaufnahmen, Hotel Palace
Luzern, Heinrich Meili-Wapf (Architekt), 1906**
Pages 8–21: Exterior and interior photographs, Hotel Palace
Lucerne, Heinrich Meili-Wapf (Architect), 1906

DIE ERÖFFNUNG DES PALACE-HOTEL IN LUZERN

Luzerner Tages-Anzeiger, Mittwoch, 9. Mai 1906, S. 2
SALU, F8, Z3:13

...gestaltete sich am Montag zu einer imposanten Feier. In den Nachmittagsstunden wanderten Hunderte von Schaulustigen am prächtigen Nationalquai hinaus, um sich das Hotel, das infolge seiner kolossalen Fassaden schon seit langem die Bewunderung der Beschauer erweckte, nun auch im Innern zu besichtigen. Als Resultat ging aus dieser Besichtigung wohl für jeden die Tatsache hervor, daß das Palace-Hotel, der Weltfirma Bucher-Durrer gehörig, heute den elegantesten und reichsten Hotels der Welt zugezählt werden darf. In unvergleichlicher Lage am See genießt man vom Garten, von den Terrassen, den Balkons die vollkommenste Aussicht auf das einzig schöne landschaftliche Bild mit dem prächtigen bergumsäumten See im Vordergrund. Die kulissenartige Stellung der Hauptfassade zum Quai selbst ermöglicht von jedem Fenster der Süd- und Westfront den ungestörten Ausblick auf die Stadt, während der Eckturm des Hotels gewissermaßen das Zentrum der radial verlaufenden Hauptstraßenzüge der Stadt bildet und von hier aus den Einblick in alle die originellen städtischen Straßenbilder gestattet. Es wirkt der Bau mit diesem kräftigen Turm als wunderbarer Abschluß des Quais.

Das Hotel trägt seinem Namen entsprechend in stolzer Einfachheit eine großzügige Fassaden-Architektur von ruhiger aber zugleich monumentaler Wirkung. In leichter Anlehnung an die moderne Richtung wurden die Barockformen im Äußern und Inneren in ausgesprochen künstlerischer Weise den zur Verwendung kommenden echten Baumaterialien angepaßt. Die Fassaden, hell gehalten, sind in Granit, Jurakalk und Savonnière-Stein ausgeführt. Die Kuppel als Abschluß des Mittelbaues ist mit Ziegeln in origineller Weise eingedeckt, während ein großartiges, in Kupfer getriebenes, oxidiertes und mächtig wirkendes Bekrönungsmotiv den Abschluß des Kuppeldaches bildet. Der weithin sichtbare Eckturm mit seiner eliptischen Grundform und dem überaus wirksamen Kuppeldach in massivem Kupfer bildet eines der künftigen Wahrzeichen der Stadt Luzern. Das Hauptportal an der Haldenstraße wird von zwei monumentalen Karyatiden dem Charakter des Hotelpalastes entsprechend flankiert. Diese sowie die verschiedenen anderen Bildhauerarbeiten sind von Hugo Siegwart in München und U. Zbinden in Luzern ausgeführt.

Im Aeußeren wurden die oben erwähnten Barockformen bei aller Freiheit streng einheitlich durchgeführt; auch die Architekturen im Innern weisen diese Stilformen auf. Immer und immer wieder begegnen wir diesen originellen Details bis auf die Möbel, Leuchter, Eßgeschirre, Gläser usw. und es darf ohne Uebertreibung gesagt werden, daß es der Erbauer dieses Riesenhotels, Hr. Architekt Meili-Wapf, meisterhaft verstanden hat, die vornehmen, für das Auge überaus wohltuenden Formen für dieses grandiose Hotel zu verwenden. Ohne Schablone und Aufdringlichkeit wurde hier ein ebenso behagliches als vornehmes Heim für Angehörige aller Nationen geschaffen, das auch den weitgehendsten Ansprüchen gerecht wird.

Das Vestibule bildet bei allem Reichtum an Marmor einen heimeligen Konzentrationspunkt für die Gäste. In feinster Weise ist das dekorative Moment sowohl im Damen- als auch im Musiksaal zum Ausdruck gekommen. Ebenso sind Speise- und Restaurationssaal und namentlich auch der American Bar in gediegenster Weise ihren Bestimmungen angepaßt.

Nicht Kopien alter Bauwerke oder ganzer Interieurs sind hier zu finden: überall tritt dem Beschauer vielmehr eigenartige Verwendung bester modernisierter Formen entgegen.

In konstruktiver Beziehung löste dieser Bau ebenfalls ein äußerst interessantes Problem. Die in ausgiebiger Weise zur Verwendung kommende armierte Betonbauweise gestattete bei größter Solidität und Feuersicherheit sowohl die Freiheit in der räumlichen Disposition als auch die vollständige Anpassung der Appartements an die Gesellschaftsräume im Parterre.

Das Hotel mit seinen 35 Salons und 250 Schlafzimmern nebst anschließenden luxuriös ausgestatteten Bade- und Toiletteräumen bildet eine Anzahl selbständiger Wohnungen, welche beliebig nach Gebrauch vergrößert oder eingeschränkt werden können, immerhin derart, daß jedes der Appartements von einem Privateingang zugänglich ist. Damit verbunden wurde erreicht, daß mit Doppelkorridor

THE OPENING OF THE PALACE HOTEL IN LUCERNE

Luzerner Tages-Anzeiger, Wednesday, May 9, 1906, p. 2
SALU, F8, Z3:13

...turned out to be an impressive celebration. In the afternoon hours, hundreds of curious members of the public wandered along the prestigious Nationalquai to take a look inside the hotel that has long inspired the awe of onlookers from outside due to its colossal façades. Following such a visit, it was no doubt clear to everyone that the Palace Hotel, owned by the global company Bucher-Durrer, can be regarded as one of the most elegant and richest hotels in the world. From the garden, terraces and balconies of this incomparable lakeside location, one enjoys the most perfect view of the uniquely beautiful landscape, with its majestic mountain-lined lake in the foreground. The backdrop-placement of the façade with respect to the quay itself enables an unhindered view of the city from every window on the south and west fronts, while the hotel's corner tower forms the centre of the city's radially running main streets, from where it affords views of all the original streetscapes. The building with this powerful tower has the effect of a wonderful conclusion to the quay.

Thus, like its name, the hotel presents the proud simplicity of its generous façade architecture, achieving a calm, yet monumental effect. In a slight reference to the modern trend, the Baroque exterior and interior forms were adapted with exquisite artistic skill to the actual building materials used. The bright façades are made of granite, Jurassic lime and Savonnière stone. The dome concluding the central section is unusually covered with tiles, while a majestic, oxidised, beaten-copper crowning motif completes the domed roof. Visible from afar, the corner tower with its basic elliptical form and the extremely effective solid-copper domed roof will be one of Lucerne's future landmarks. The main portal on Halden-strasse is flanked by two monumental caryatids, which are appropriate to the character of the Palace Hotel. These and various other sculptures were produced by Hugo Siegwart in Munich and U. Zbinden in Lucerne.

Despite all of its freedoms, the above-mentioned Baroque exterior forms were produced in strict uniformity; the architecture inside also presents the same stylistic forms. One constantly encounters the original details, down to the furniture, lights, crockery, glasses etc. and it is no exaggeration to say that the builder of this enormous hotel, the architect Meili-Wapf, has a masterful grasp of forms for this superb hotel, which are refined and pleasing to the eye. Without being mimicking or obtrusive, the result is a comfortable and noble home for citizens of all nations, fulfilling even the most strenuous demands.

Despite the wealth of marble, the vestibule forms a cosy gathering point for the hotel guests. Decorative elements are exquisitely presented both in the ladies' salon and the music hall. Similarly, the dining and restaurant hall, as well as the American Bar, have been elegantly adapted to their allocated functions.

Instead of seeing copies of old buildings or entire interiors, the viewer finds unusual uses for the finest, modernised forms everywhere.

With respect to its construction, the building also solved an extremely interesting problem. The large-scale use of reinforced concrete ensured exceptional solidity and fire-safety, while also enabling free spatial arrangement and allowing complete adaptation of the social space on the ground floor.

The hotel, with its 35 suites and 250 bedrooms, including luxuriously decorated adjoining bathroom and toilet facilities, offers a number of autonomous apartments that can be freely expanded or partitioned, while providing each apartment with a private entrance. To that aim, the hotel excellently uses the double corridor to shield guests from any noises that the hotel operations might cause.

This exquisite solution fulfils the most demanding requirements and is a sight to be seen in the field of modern hotel buildings.

No expense has been spared in terms of the guests' comfort, including lifts installed in the vestibule; furthermore, the hotel offers a post office, a telephone cubicle, a kiosk selling books and magazines, a typewriter room etc. The basement accommodates a hair-dresser's salon and a billiards room.

A new hygiene feature that is not to be underestimated is the so-called vacuum cleaner.

In the evening, a select society of friends of the Bucher family, hoteliers, suppliers and press representatives gathered in the halls, which were festively lit for the first time. During the delicious dinner, Mr Fritz Bucher welcomed the guests in the name of the Swiss

der Gast von jedem Geräusch, welches der Hotelbetrieb mit sich bringt, in tadelloser Weise abgeschlossen ist.

Diese vorzügliche Lösung ermöglicht es, den weitgehendsten Bedürfnissen zu entsprechen und bildet eine Sehenswürdigkeit auf dem Gebiete des modernen Hotelbaues.

Auch in anderer Richtung ist der Bequemlichkeit der Gäste in reichstem Masse Rechnung getragen durch Anbringung von Lifts im Vestibule; vorhanden sind ferner ein Postbureau, eine Telephon-Kabine, Bücher- und Zeitungskiosk, Schreibmaschinenzimmer. Im Souterrain befindet sich Coiffeur- und Billard-Salon.

Als neue nicht zu unterschätzende Einrichtung vom hygienischen Standpunkt aus ist ein sogen. Vacuum-Cleaner (Staubsauger, Reiniger) zu erwähnen.

In den zum ersten Mal festlich erleuchteten Sälen bewegte sich abends eine gewählte Gesellschaft von Freunden der Familie Bucher, von Hoteliers, Lieferanten und Vertretern der Presse. Während dem mit feinstem Geschmack servierten Diner begrüßte Herr Fritz Bucher im Namen der Schweiz. Hotelgesellschaft die Eingeladenen. In verbindlicher Weise brachte er dem Erbauer des Palace seinen Dank entgegen und gegenüber seinen Herren Kollegen betonte er, daß das neue Haus nicht der Konkurrenz, sondern dem Fremdenverkehr, dem Blühen und Gedeihen Luzerns dienen soll. Herr Emil Spillmann brachte einen kernigen Trinkspruch auf die Kollegialität der Hoteliers aus, auf die Familie Bucher und ihren genialen Chef den Papa Bucher-Durrer. Oberst Geißhüsler begrüßte das Hotel als neue reiche Verdienstquelle für den Handelsstand, Herr Nat.-Rat Bucher pries in geistreichen humorvollen Worten die Solidarität der Hoteliers und der übrigen Bevölkerung.

Gegen 11 Uhr erst war das prunkvolle Mahl in Süßigkeit und Schaumwein ausgeklungen. Die temperamentvollen Weisen des italienischen Hotelorchesters wurden jetzt vom Geknatter eines Feuerwerkes abgelöst, dessen Lichtgarben von dem zahlreichen Publikum, das sich den ganzen Abend schon das hell beleuchtete Hotel angesehen, mit lebhaftem Beifall aufgenommen wurden.

hotel company. He expressed his profound thanks to the builder of the Palace, while stressing to his colleagues that the new building is not intended as competition, but as a contribution to the enhancement and prosperity of Lucerne. Mr Emil Spillmann raised a hearty toast to the hoteliers' collegiality, the Bucher Family and its congenial head, Papa Bucher-Durrer. Colonel Geißhüsler welcomed the hotel as a rich new source of income for the business sector, while Mr Bucher chose intelligently humorous words to praise the solidarity of the hotel sector and the rest of the public.

Around 11 o'clock, the splendid meal ended with sweets and sparkling wine. The spirited tunes of the Italian hotel orchestra were replaced by the crackle of fireworks, their shimmering lights earning lively applause from the numerous members of the public that had come to look at the brightly lit hotel throughout the evening.

DAS HOTEL PALACE ZU SEINER ENTSTEHUNGSZEIT

Peter Omachen

Die Verwandlung hätte grösser nicht sein können: An einer damals noch wenig be-
fahrenen Ausfallstrasse am Stadtrand von Luzern – dort, wo sich zuvor der Lager-
platz eines Bauunternehmens am Seeufer ausbreitete – entstand 1904 bis 1906 das
Hotel Palace. «Es ist mit einem Wort ein architektonisches Meisterwerk»[1], das «den
elegantesten und reichsten Hotels der Welt zugezählt werden darf»[2], brachte die
Luzerner Presse ihre begeisterte Berichterstattung nach der Einweihung vom 7. Mai
1906 auf den Punkt. Der luxuriöse Hotelbau bildete den vorläufigen Höhepunkt der
sogenannten Tourismusindustrie, die sich seit dem frühen 19. Jahrhundert in Luzern
entwickelt hatte.[3]

LUZERN UND DER TOURISMUS

Nicht der Stadt wegen kamen die ersten Touristen nach Luzern, es war die idyllische
Lage am Rande der Voralpen und am See, die die neuen «Lustreisenden» lockte.
Erst die Aufklärung hatte die Verbindung von Reisen und Freizeit hervorgebracht.
Zuvor war das Reisen den Händlern und Pilgern, Soldaten und Handwerkern, den
Reisenden in politischer Mission oder auf dem Weg zur Bäderkur vorbehalten ge-
wesen. Es waren vornehmlich Aristokratensöhne aus dem Norden, zumeist aus
England, die im 18. Jahrhundert auf ihre «Grand Tour» nach Italien geschickt wurden
und dabei auch die Schweiz kennenlernten. Die Wahrnehmung der Gebirgszüge der
Alpen, zuvor Orte der Entbehrung, des Schreckens und der Hässlichkeit, wandelte
sich in den Augen der jungen Romantiker zum Inbegriff von Schönheit und Reinheit.

  Da diese ersten Touristen und ihre Begleiter noch in geringer Anzahl unter-
wegs waren, reichte vorerst das althergebrachte Angebot an Unterkünften und
Transportmitteln aus. Erst 1782 wurde mit dem Hotel Zum Goldenen Adler am
Hirschenplatz ein erstes Gasthaus in Luzern baulich an die neuen Gästebedürfnisse
angepasst und vergrössert. Das Hotel des Balances war 1810 das erste Hotel am
Wasser, nämlich an der Reuss, und mit Blick auf die Berge. Das erste Hotel am See
schliesslich war der Schwanen, der nach einem Brand 1835 aus der Altstadt an den
heutigen, später nach ihm benannten Schwanenplatz verlegt wurde. Der Schwanen
war allerdings ebenfalls noch kein eigenständiger Hotelneubau, sondern lediglich der
Umbau und die Vergrösserung eines vormaligen Wohnhauses. Das erste, eigens zu
diesem Zweck errichtete touristische Hotel war schliesslich der Schweizerhof von
1845.

  Zunächst war es also nur eine kleine, privilegierte Bevölkerungsschicht, die
sich das Reisen als Freizeitvergnügen überhaupt leisten konnte. Entsprechend waren
die ersten Häuser durchwegs Hotels der Luxusklasse. Der fünfwöchige Ferienauf-
enthalt von Königin Victoria von England 1868 machte Luzern endgültig zum bevor-
zugten Ziel der internationalen Hautevolee. Durch den wirtschaftlichen Aufschwung
und die Mechanisierung des Reisens wurden Ferien im letzten Viertel des 19. Jahrhunderts für immer grössere Bevölkerungskreise möglich. In der Belle Époque, also
in der Zeitspanne vom Ende des Deutsch-Französischen Krieges 1873 bis zum Aus-
bruch des Ersten Weltkriegs 1914, beschleunigte sich das touristische Wachstum
rasant. Es entstanden zahlreiche Hotelum- und -neubauten, aber auch einfache Um-
nutzungen von bestehenden Wohnhäusern zu Fremdenpensionen. Mit Einführung
der Druckwasserversorgung ab 1875 eroberten die Hotelbetriebe zunehmend auch
die Hänge über der Stadt mit ihrer hervorragenden Aussicht. Vor dem Ersten Weltkrieg beherbergte Luzern mit seinen rund 40 000 Einwohnerinnen und Einwohnern
jährlich knapp 200 000 Gäste mit mehr als einer halben Million Logiernächten in
über 100 Hotels und Pensionen.

  Nach den Hotels Schweizerhof 1845 und National 1870 war das Hotel Palace
1906 das dritte und bis heute jüngste «Erstklasshotel» in der Stadt Luzern. Es steht
zusammen mit den beiden anderen Fünf-Sterne-Hotels am Luzerner Seebecken.
Während beim Schweizerhof die Strasse noch vor dem Hotel verläuft, verfügen das
National und das Palace über eine rückwärtige Strassenerschliessung und profitieren
somit von einer privilegierten Lage direkt am Wasser. Einzig die Quaianlage mit
ihrer Kastanienallee trennt die beiden Hotelbauten vom See. Diese öffentlichen

THE HOTEL PALACE AT THE TIME OF ITS CONSTRUCTION

Peter Omachen

The transformation could hardly have been greater: the Hotel Palace was built between 1904 and 1906 beside what was then a quiet arterial road on the outskirts of Lucerne – on the site of a building company's storage area spreading out along the lake shore. "In a word, we have an architectural masterpiece before us,"[1] that, "can be regarded as one of the most elegant and richest hotels in the world,"[2] as the Lucerne press concluded in its enthusiastic reports following the hotel's inauguration on May 7, 1906. The luxurious hotel building represented the initial climax of what had become known as the tourist industry, which had been developing in Lucerne since the early 19th century.[3]

LUCERNE AND TOURISM

The first tourists came not for the city, but to experience its idyllic location on the edge of the Alpine foothills and by the lake that was so appealing to the new "pleasure travellers". The Age of Enlightenment had stressed a connection between travel and freedom. Before then, it had been a necessary activity for merchants, pilgrims, soldiers and craftsmen, as well as travellers with a political mission, or patients seeking to be cured in a spa. Initially, the new 18th-century travellers were aristocratic sons from the North, mostly from England, who were sent to Italy on their "grand tour", passing through Switzerland on the way. Their perception of the Alps, previously regarded as a place of deprivation, trepidation and ugliness, transformed in the eyes of young Romantics into the epitome of beauty and purity.

Since these first tourists and their accompanying parties still travelled in small numbers, it was initially sufficient to provide them with traditional facilities for accommodation and transport. It was only in 1782 that the first establishment in Lucerne, the Hotel Zum Goldenen Adler am Hirschenplatz, was structurally adapted and expanded to accommodate the guests' new requirements. Opened in 1810, the Hotel des Balances became the first of its kind at a waterside location, by the River Reuss, affording a view of the mountains. The first lakeside hotel was the Schwanen, which was relocated from the old town following a fire in 1835 and subsequently situated on the square that would later be renamed Schwanenplatz. However, the Schwanen was still not an autonomous, new hotel building, since it was based on a converted and extended former residential building. In 1845, the Schweizerhof became the first tourist hotel specifically constructed for that purpose.

Initially, only a small privileged class could afford to travel for pleasure and the first hotels were all appropriately luxurious. When England's Queen Victoria resided in Lucerne for five weeks in 1868, the city finally became a preferred destination for the international elite. During the last quarter of the 19th century, economic prosperity and the mechanisation of travel made holidays possible for an ever-growing proportion of society. The tourist industry boomed during the Belle Époque, which lasted from 1873, after the end of the Franco-Prussian War, to the outbreak of World War I in 1914. Numerous hotels were converted or newly built. Sometimes, existing residential buildings were simply transformed into tourist boarding houses. The introduction of a pressured water supply in 1875 allowed hotels to be built on the sloping terrain overlooking the city, with their magnificent views. Prior to World War I, Lucerne had around 40,000 inhabitants and almost 200,000 guests a year, generating more than half a million overnight stays in over 100 hotels and boarding houses.

Following the Hotel Schweizerhof in 1845 and the National Hotel in 1870, the Hotel Palace became the city of Lucerne's third "first class" hotel in 1906 and remains its newest to this day. It stands together with the other five-star establishments on Lucerne's lake basin. While the Hotel Schweizerhof is situated behind the lakeside road, the National and the Palace have rear-side access to it and thereby benefit from a privileged location directly by the water. Only the public quay with its chestnut promenade separates the hotel from the lake. These public open spaces were created together with the hotel: the Schweizerhofquai with the opening of the Hotel Schweizerhof, and its extension, the Nationalquai after the Hotel National opened. This shows how important the status of these private businesses has always been in public perception and with respect to Lucerne's public spaces. Before the Hotel Palace was built, the quay running along the natural shoreline extended up to the property's boundary. The section in front of the building was also raised when the hotel was built, while the public lakeside promenade was only extended out of the city at a later date.

Die Haldenstrasse um 1870. Hinten links das Hotel Beau-Rivage (erbaut 1867). Das Hotel Palace entstand später an der Strassenbiegung schräg gegenüber.
Haldenstrasse around 1870. Hotel Beau-Rivage (built in 1867, rear left). Hotel Palace was built later on the diagonally opposite bend in the road.

Freiräume sind jeweils zusammen mit den Hotels entstanden: Der Schweizerhof-quai gleichzeitig mit dem Hotel Schweizerhof und seine Verlängerung, der National-quai, zusammen mit dem Hotel National. Dies zeigt, wie wichtig die Stellung dieser Privatbetriebe in der öffentlichen Wahrnehmung und im öffentlichen Raum immer schon war. Vor der Entstehung des Hotel Palace reichte der dem natürlichen Ufer vorgelagerte Quai bis an dessen Grundstücksgrenze. Auch hier wurde mit dem Bau des Hotels das Teilstück vor dem Gebäude aufgeschüttet. Erst später setzte man die öffentlichen Seeuferanlagen weiter stadtauswärts fort.

1903 war es der Schweizerischen Hotelgesellschaft unter der Leitung des Obwaldner Unternehmers Franz Josef Bucher-Durrer gelungen, dieses 3 285 Qua-dratmeter grosse Grundstück an der Haldenstrasse zwischen den Tennisplätzen beim Kursaal und der damaligen Pension Kaufmann für 880 000 Franken zu erwer-ben. Zwischen Juni 1904 und Mai 1906 wurde für die damals astronomische Summe von rund 3,4 Millionen Franken ein Hotelbau der Spitzenklasse erstellt, der keine Wünsche offenliess.

DER ARCHITEKT UND SEIN BAUHERR

Der Architekt dieses viel gerühmten Baus war Heinrich Meili-Wapf (1860–1927). Er hatte in seiner Heimatstadt Zürich am Eidgenössischen Polytechnikum (heute ETH Zürich) Architektur studiert. Nach Wanderjahren in Wien, Budapest, Triest und Florenz kam er 1889 nach Luzern, wo er auf Vermittlung seines Professors Friedrich Bluntschli im Architekturbüro von Arnold Bringolf Arbeit fand. Noch im selben Jahr heiratete er die Pianistin Emilie Wapf und im Jahr darauf gründete er sein eigenes Architekturbüro. 1892 bis 1898 war er Chef der Hochbauabteilung der Gotthard-bahn, für die er mehrere Bahnhöfe baute. Durch eine Reihe von Wettbewerbserfol-gen, etwa dem 1. Preis für die Kantonsschule in Schaffhausen, wurde der junge Ar-chitekt in der ganzen Schweiz bekannt. Sein preisgekrönter Stadtbauplan von 1895 beeinflusste die städtebauliche Entwicklung von Luzern massgeblich. Darüber hin-aus setzte Meili-Wapf mit zahlreichen Wohnbauten wichtige Akzente im Stadtbild. 1900 lehne er eine Berufung als Professor ans Technikum Winterthur ab. Er war Mitglied des Grossen Stadtrats von Luzern und Präsident von dessen Baukommis-sion. Zu seinen bekanntesten Arbeiten zählen die im Auftrag der Schweizerischen Hotelgesellschaft des Unternehmers Franz Josef Bucher-Durrer erstellten Hotel-bauten, nämlich das 1903/04 erstellte Hotel Palace auf dem Bürgenstock, das Palace in Luzern sowie das 1907 eröffnete Hotel Semiramis in Kairo (abgebrochen 1976).[4]

Heinrich Meili-Wapf führte sein Architekturbüro von 1917 bis zur Aufgabe seiner Berufstätigkeit 1924 zusammen mit seinem Sohn Armin Meili, der später selbst ein berühmter Architekt werden sollte. Im Nachruf schrieb dieser 1927 über seinen Vater: «Die äussere Schale schien manchmal hart; wie das Edelmetall tief in den Adern des Gesteins verborgen liegt, so war zu dem Golde seines Herzens nicht so leicht zu dringen.»

Einen völlig anderen Start ins Berufsleben hatte der Unternehmer und Bau-herr des Hotel Palace in Luzern, Franz Josef Bucher-Durrer (1834–1906). Er war als Bauernsohn im Kanton Obwalden aufgewachsen, wo er zunächst die Dorfschule in Kerns und 1844/45 die Realschule am Kollegium Sarnen besuchte. Als Ältester von fünf Geschwistern musste er nach dem Tod seines Vaters bereits mit 15 Jahren zu-sammen mit der Mutter die Leitung des elterlichen Betriebes übernehmen. Nach Jahren als Alpsenn und Bauer gründete er 1864 mit seinem zukünftigen Schwager Josef Durrer die Firma Bucher & Durrer, die zunächst Sägereien betrieb. 1868 grün-deten sie in Kägiswil eine Parkettfabrik und erstellten Scheunen und Wohnhäuser. 1869/70 bauten sie ihr erstes Hotel, den Sonnenberg in Engelberg. Mit dem Ver-kaufserlös erwarben Bucher & Durrer im Jahr darauf die Trittalp auf dem Bürgen-berg, wo sie das Grand Hotel Bürgenstock errichteten, das 1873 mit grossem Erfolg eröffnet und 1887 bis 1905 zu einem weitläufigen Hotelkomplex, unter anderem mit elektrischer Standseilbahn, Park- und Palace-Hotel sowie dem Hammetschwandlift, erweitert wurde.

Ab Anfang der 1880er-Jahre war die Firma unter der Leitung Josef Durrers auf dem Gebiet des Holzhandels und der Holzverarbeitung in Südosteuropa tätig. Franz Josef Bucher-Durrer leitete den Hotelzweig, der sich ab 1879, vor allem aber in den 1890er-Jahren in der Schweiz und im Ausland zu einer beeindruckenden Erst-klasshotel-Kette entwickelte, unter anderem mit dem Grandhotel Méditerranée in

Der Bauplatz wird vorbereitet: Abtransport eines Holzgebäudes an der Stelle des späteren Hotel Palace. Links das damalige Ende des Nationalquais, im Hintergrund die Hotels Belvédère (erbaut 1896) und Eden (erbaut 1894). Foto 1904.
Building-site preparation: removal of a wooden building at the location of the later Hotel Palace. Left, the former end of the Nationalquai; in the background, Hotel Belvédère (built in 1896) and Hotel Eden (built in 1894). Photo taken in 1904.

Bauarbeiter posieren vor der Holzschalung und den Armierungseisen des «Systems Hennebique», der erst wenige Jahre zuvor erfundenen Eisenbetonkonstruktion. Foto Baustelle Hotel Palace um 1905
Building workers pose in front of the wooden formwork and the reinforcing iron of the „Hennebique system", a reinforced structure that had only been invented a few years earlier. Photo of the building site around 1905.

Das Hotel Semiramis in Kairo (Ägypten) unmittelbar vor seiner Fertigstellung 1907. Die grossformatige Bautafel wirbt für die «Bucher-Durrer Hotels».
Semiramis Hotel in Cairo (Egypt) just before its completion in 1907. The large-scale building sign advertises the "Bucher-Durrer hotels".

In 1903, the Schweizerische Hotelgesellschaft, directed by the Obwalden-based entrepreneur Franz Josef Bucher-Durrer, purchased the 3,285 square metre property on Haldenstrasse between the tennis courts by the Kursaal and what was then the Pension Kaufmann, at a price of 880,000 Franks. Between June 1904 and May 1906, a new top-class hotel was constructed at the astronomical cost of around 3.4 million Franks, leaving no wishes unfulfilled.

THE ARCHITECT AND HIS CLIENT

The architect of this widely renowned building was Heinrich Meili-Wapf (1860–1927). He had studied Architecture in his home town of Zurich at the Eidgenössisches Polytechnikum (today's ETH Zurich). After gathering experience in Vienna, Budapest, Triest and Florence, he came to Lucerne in 1889, where he was employed at the architectural office of Arnold Bringolf following a recommendation by his professor, Friedrich Bluntschli. The same year, he married the pianist Emilie Wapf, before founding his own architectural office a year later. From 1892 to 1898, he was Head of the Structural Engineering Department at the Gotthardbahn, designing several railway stations for the company. A series of competition successes, such as 1st Prize for the Cantonal School in Schaffhausen, made the young architect renowned throughout Switzerland. His prize-winning urban plan in 1895 had a decisive influence on Lucerne's urban development. Furthermore, Meili-Wapf added highlights to the cityscape with numerous residential buildings. In 1900, he turned down an appointment as Professor at the Technikum Winterthur. He was a member of the Greater Urban Council of Lucerne and President of its Building Committee. His most famous works include the hotel buildings contracted by the Schweizerische Hotelgesellschaft, namely the Bürgenstock Hotel Palace built in 1903/04, the Palace in Lucerne and the Semiramis Hotel in Cairo, which opened in 1907 (and was demolished in 1976).[4]

Heinrich Meili-Wapf managed his architectural office from 1917 until his retirement in 1924, together with his son Armin Meili, who later himself became a famous architect. In an obituary he wrote about his father in 1927, Armin Meili wrote: "The outer shell sometimes seemed hard; just as lodes of precious metals lie hidden deep within the rock, it was not so easy to reach his heart of gold."

Franz Josef Bucher-Durrer (1834–1906), the entrepreneur and builder of the Hotel Palace in Lucerne, had a completely different start to his professional career. He grew up as a farmer's son in the Canton of Obwalden, where he initially attended the village school in Kerns, before joining the secondary school at the Kollegium Sarnen in 1844/45. The eldest of five siblings, he was just 15 years old when his father died, forcing him to take over management of the family business together with his mother. In 1864, after spending years as an Alpine shepherd and farmer, he joined forces with his future brother-in-law Josef Durrer and founded the company Bucher & Durrer, which initially operated sawmills. In 1868, they founded a parquet factory in Kägiswil, which also produced barns and residential buildings. In 1869/70, they built their first hotel, the Sonnenberg in Engelberg. The following year, Bucher & Durrer used the profits generated by the hotel's sale to purchase Alp Tritt on the Bürgenstock, where the company built the Grand Hotel Bürgenstock, which was immediately successful after opening in 1873. The hotel was expanded between 1887 and 1905 into an extensive complex, including an electric funicular railway, the Park Hotel, the Palace Hotel and the Hammetschwandlift.

From the early 1880s onwards, the company was managed by Josef Durrer and entered the field of trading and processing timber in southern Europe. Franz Josef Bucher-Durrer managed the hotel department, which, from 1879 onwards and especially in the 1890s, developed an impressive chain of first class hotels in Switzerland and abroad, including the Grandhotel Méditerranée in Pegli near Genoa and the Hotel de l'Europe in Lucerne, as well as the Hotel Minerva and the Hotel Quirinal in Rome. From the mid-1880s, the company was also active in tram building, with projects in Lugano, Genoa and elsewhere, as well as building mountain railways, for instance on Mount Stanserhorn and the Monte San Salvatore. The company's broad range of activities even extended to building electric power stations.

The company was dissolved in 1895. Franz Josef Bucher-Durrer took over the hotels and mountain railways, founded the Schweizerische Hotelgesellschaft in 1900 and built more luxury hotels in its name: the Palace in Lugano in 1900, the Palace in Milan in 1902, followed by the Palace in Lucerne and the Semiramis in Cairo. His entrepreneurial skill and impressive dynamism made him a "hotel king" millionaire. He was a Councillor in Kerns and Obwalden Cantonal Councillor from 1884 to 1896, as well as initiating, co-founding and co-managing

Pegli bei Genua, dem Hotel de l'Europe in Luzern und den Hotels Minerva und Quirinal in Rom. Zudem betätigte sich das Unternehmen ab Mitte der 1880er-Jahre im Bereich des Strassenbahnbaus, unter anderem in Lugano und Genua, sowie der Erstellung von Bergbahnen, etwa auf das Stanserhorn und auf den Monte San Salvatore. Sogar der Bau von Elektrizitätswerken gehörte zum breiten Tätigkeitsfeld.

1895 wurde die Firma aufgelöst. Franz Josef Bucher-Durrer übernahm die Hotels und Bergbahnen, gründete 1900 die Schweizerische Hotelgesellschaft und baute in deren Namen weitere Luxushotels: 1900 das Palace in Lugano, 1902 das Palace in Mailand, danach das Palace in Luzern und das Semiramis in Kairo. Mit Unternehmergeist und beeindruckendem Elan arbeitete er sich zum millionenschweren «Hotelkönig» empor. Er war Gemeinderat in Kerns, 1884 bis 1896 Obwaldner Kantonsrat sowie Initiant, Mitbegründer und Verwaltungsrat der 1886 gegründeten Obwaldner Kantonalbank. Er starb am 6. Oktober 1906 kurz vor der Eröffnung des Hotel Semiramis.[5]

DER URSPRÜNGLICHE BAU

Bei seiner Eröffnung 1906 präsentierte sich das Hotel Palace als fünfgeschossiger Baukörper unter einem von Kuppeln und Giebeln bekrönten Mansarddach. Mit seinen rund 82 Metern Länge, 23 Metern Breite und 27 Metern Höhe bildete der wuchtige Hotelbau von Anbeginn an einen markanten Merkpunkt im Stadtbild von Luzern. Der damalige Haupteingang lag in der Fassadenmitte an der Haldenstrasse, von wo aus eine innenliegende Treppe ein halbes Geschoss hinauf zum Hochparterre führte. An das zentrale Vestibül schlossen ostseitig der Speisesaal, der auch als Festsaal des Hotels benutzt wurde, sowie das zum See hin orientierte Restaurant an. Der Unterschied zwischen diesen beiden Angeboten lag im Service: Während im Speisesaal zu einer bestimmten Uhrzeit eine festgelegte Menüfolge serviert wurde, konnte im exklusiveren Restaurant à la carte bestellt werden. Diese um 1900 in der Luxushotellerie eingeführte Neuerung bedingte einen grösseren und aufwändigeren Küchenbetrieb, der im Tiefparterre untergebracht und über Diensttreppen und Speiselifte mit den beiden Offices neben den Essälen verbunden war.

Auf der Westseite des Hotels lagen zum See hin verschiedene Aufenthaltsräume, nämlich der Lesesaal, der Damensaal, der Musiksaal und die Bar. In diesen Räumen spielte sich das gesellschaftliche Leben der damaligen Hotelgäste ab. Ihr Aufenthalt dehnte sich oft über mehrere Wochen aus und der gesellschaftliche Austausch hatte in diesem sozialen Umfeld einen hohen Stellenwert. Strassenseitig, westlich neben dem Haupteingang, befand sich die Verwaltung, gefolgt von der Direktionswohnung an der stadtseitigen Haldenstrassenecke. Der Hoteldirektor hatte von dieser strategisch günstigen Position aus jederzeit die ankommenden Gäste im Blick, die mit der hoteleigenen Limousine am Bahnhof abgeholt wurden. Es gehörte zu seinen Aufgaben, die wichtigen Gäste bei ihrer Ankunft persönlich zu begrüssen.

Über dem damaligen Haupteingang stieg das lichtdurchflutete dreiläufige Treppenhaus mit gegenüberliegendem Lift als Rückgrat des Hauses bis zum ersten Dachgeschoss hinauf. Das zweite Dachgeschoss enthielt Personalzimmer und Abstellräume. Das Gebäude längs durchlaufende Korridore erschlossen die Zimmeretagen. Diese Gänge lagen nicht in der Mittelachse des Baukörpers, sondern waren gegen die Haldenstrasse versetzt angeordnet, so dass die Räume mit Aussicht gegen den See möglichst viel Platz erhielten. Entlang der seeseitigen Hauptfassade waren durch Türen miteinander verbundene Schlafzimmer und Salons aneinandergereiht, gefolgt von einer inneren Erschliessungszone mit privaten Bädern und Kammern für die Dienerschaft. Diese lagen an sieben Licht- und Belüftungsschächten, welche auch die Korridore mit Tageslicht versorgten. Alle Zimmer auf der Seeseite verfügten über ein eigenes Privatbad. Dieser Sanitärkomfort galt damals als ungeheurer Luxus: Erst wenige Jahre zuvor, 1898, hatte der aus dem Wallis stammende Hotelier César Ritz erstmals Privatbäder zu jedem Zimmer in seinem Hotel Ritz in Paris eingerichtet.

Zusammen mit der Einführung von Privatbädern war das sogenannte «Appartementsystem» um 1900 entwickelt worden und hatte sich in den folgenden Jahren in der Luxushotellerie durchgesetzt. Es richtete sich an eine Klientel, die oft wochen- und monatelang Aufenthalt nahm und zum Teil mit eigenem Hauspersonal reiste. Es ermöglichte die freie Kombination beliebig vieler Schlaf-, Wohn- und Sanitärräume zu individuellen Suiten, die je nach Wunsch und Bedarf der Gäste zusammengestellt

Das Hotel Palace unmittelbar nach seiner Fertigstellung 1906. Links hinter den Alleebäumen die Tennisplätze des Kursaals, rechts die neu erstelle Fortsetzung des Quais. Dahinter die Pension Kaufmann (erbaut 1862, abgebrochen 1978).
The Hotel Palace immediately after its completion in 1906. The Kursaal tennis courts are visible to the left, behind the avenue trees. The newly built extension to the quay runs to the right. Pension Kaufmann (built in 1862, demolished in 1978) is situated behind it.

Der Hoteleingang, 1906
Hotel entrance, 1906

the Obwaldner Kantonalbank, which was founded in 1886. He died on October 6, 1906 shortly before the Hotel Semiramis was opened.[5]

THE ORIGINAL BUILDING

When it opened in 1906, the Hotel Palace revealed its five-storey volume beneath a mansard roof, crowned with domes and gables. From the outset, the massive building's 82-metre length, 23-metre width and 27-metre height made it a striking landmark in Lucerne's cityscape. The main entrance at the time was situated at the centre of the façade on the Haldenstrasse side, from where an interior staircase led up half a storey to the mezzanine level. The central vestibule was connected to the dining hall to the east, which was also used for the hotel's festivities, and the restaurant orientated towards the lake. The difference between these two facilities lay in the service: while a fixed menu was served at specific times in the dining hall, the exclusive restaurant served à la carte orders. This innovation to the luxury hotel business was introduced in 1900, requiring larger and more work-intensive cuisine operations, which were accommodated in the basement and connected to the two offices beside the dining rooms via service stairs and dumb waiters.

The hotel's west side, facing the lake, accommodated various communal rooms, namely the reading room, the ladies' salon, the music room and the bar. This is where the hotel's social life thrived. Guests often stayed for several weeks and social interaction had a high status in that social environment. The administration was situated on the street side to the west of the main entrance, followed by the Director's apartment on the town-side corner of Haldenstrasse. The hotel's Director had a strategically advantageous position from where he could always see arriving guests, who were driven from the station in the hotel's own limousine. It was his responsibility to greet important guests personally on their arrival.

The brightly lit, triple-flight stairs led up from the main entrance to the attic level, with an opposite lift, forming the building's backbone. The second attic level accommodated staff boarding and storage spaces. The corridors running longitudinally through the building serviced the floors with guest rooms. These corridors were not situated on the central axis of the building and instead placed closer to Haldenstrasse, allowing the rooms with a view of the lake to be as spacious as possible. Along the main lakeside façade, bedrooms and salons were connected by doors, followed by an inner access zone with private bathrooms and chambers for domestic staff. They were situated beside seven shafts providing light and ventilation, while naturally illuminating the corridors. All rooms on the lake side had their own private bathrooms. Such sanitary convenience was considered an incredible luxury at the time: in 1898, only a few years earlier, the Wallis-based hotelier César Ritz had been the first to introduce private bathrooms to every room in his Parisian Ritz Hotel.

Around 1900, a further innovation complemented the private bathrooms, namely the "apartment system", which subsequently became established in luxury hotels. It was aimed at a clientele that often stayed for weeks or months, sometimes bringing their own domestic staff. The system made it possible to freely combine several bedrooms, living rooms and bathrooms into individual suites, which could be arranged as required. The price of an individual apartment room could be ten times the price of a simple single room, not to mention the price of an entire individualised suite. The apartment system led to extensive hotel brochures presenting floor plans with prices of individual rooms, allowing precise reservations.

The southwestern corner on the hotel's town side contained permanently furnished suites with four or five rooms and a salon in the oval corner tower. The "simple guest rooms" were situated on the building's rear side towards the east. These only had shared bathrooms on each floor.

The building also used state of the art technology and engineering: the shell construction was built according to the "Hennebique system". This first reinforced-concrete structure was suitable for buildings and had been patented by Franzose François Hennebique in 1892. After the turn of the century, it went on to conquer the global construction industry. The revolutionary building material was first used in Central Switzerland in 1900 for the extension to the Hotel National. The Hotel Palace was still a very early example of a concrete building in Switzerland. The technique made it possible to span large ground-floor spaces using thin ceilings and, unlike wood, was regarded as fire-resistant and hygienic.

The façades of the Hotel Palace reveal the beginning transformation in architectural approaches after the turn of the century. The building's composition is still orientated towards traditional forms: a five-winged volume, structured by a central avant-corps with a

werden konnten. Der Preis eines einzelnen Appartement-Zimmers konnte gegenüber einem einfachen Fremdenzimmer bis zum Zehnfachen betragen, ganz zu schweigen vom Preis einer ganzen Zimmerfolge. Das Appartementsystem brachte umfangreiche Hotelprospekte mit sich, in denen auf Etagenplänen der Preis jedes einzelnen Zimmers ausgezeichnet war und die präzise Reservierungen ermöglichten.

Die stadtseitige Südwestecke des Hotels enthielt fest eingerichtete Suiten mit vier bis fünf Zimmern und einem Salon im ovalen Eckturm. An der Gebäuderückseite und nach Osten lagen die «einfacheren Fremdenzimmer», die nur über Etagenbäder verfügten.

Auch auf der technischen Seite war das Gebäude auf der Höhe seiner Zeit: Der Rohbau wurde nach dem «Hennebique-System» errichtet. So nannte sich die erste gebäudetaugliche Eisenbeton-Konstruktion, die der Franzose François Hennebique 1892 hatte patentieren lassen und die nach der Jahrhundertwende ihren weltweiten Siegeszug im Bauwesen antrat. Nach der erstmaligen Anwendung dieses revolutionären neuen Baustoffs in der Zentralschweiz bei der Erweiterung des Hotel National 1900, ist das Hotel Palace immer noch ein sehr frühes Beispiel eines Betonbaus in der Schweiz. Diese Technik erlaubte etwa das Überspannen der grossen Erdgeschossräume mit dünnen Geschossdecken und galt im Gegensatz zu Holz als feuerhemmende und hygienisch einwandfreie Konstruktion.

Die Fassaden des Hotel Palace lassen den sich nach der Jahrhundertwende abzeichnenden Wandel in der Architekturauffassung bereits erahnen. So orientierte sich die Komposition des Gebäudes noch an traditionellen Formen: fünfteiliger Baukörper, gegliedert durch Mittelrisalit mit Welscher Haube, zwei Seitenrisalite, erhöhtes Sockelgeschoss mit massivem Bossenquadermauerwerk, drei hierarchisch gegliederte Zimmergeschosse und Mansarddachabschluss. Im Detail lassen sich aber zahlreiche Abweichungen vom traditionellen Formenkanon erkennen; bereits im Grundriss fehlt die Symmetrie der beiden Seitenrisalite, auch in der Fassaden- und Dachgestaltung unterscheiden sich die beiden seeseitigen Gebäudeecken deutlich. Mit Giebel, kuppelartigem Dachaufsatz und Turm wird die Silhouette effektvoll aufgelockert. Durch den stadtseitigen Eckturm erhält das Palace zudem seine unverwechselbare Gestalt.

Für die Fassaden übernimmt Meili-Wapf traditionelle Elemente wie die Wandpilaster in den Risaliten sowie Lisenen und Kapitelle. Das eigentliche Dekor weist hingegen mit seinen floralen Formen Einflüsse des Jugendstils auf. Die zahlreichen plastischen Bildhauerarbeiten an der Fassade wurden durch die bekannten Künstler Hugo Siegwart und Joseph Zbinden ausgeführt.

WÜRDIGUNG

Von weither sichtbar steht das Hotel Palace als dominanter Baukörper an den Luzerner Quaianlagen. Zusammen mit dem weiter stadteinwärts liegenden Hotel National und dem zwischen den beiden Hotelbetrieben positionierten Kursaal bildet es eine markante Dreiergruppe prominenter Tourismusbauten am Luzerner Seebecken. Der Bau ist umgeben von weiteren ehemaligen und zum Teil heute noch bestehenden Hotelbetrieben aus der Zeit der Belle Époque, die jedoch alle bergseitig der uferbegleitenden Haldenstrasse angeordnet sind.

Das Palace gehört zum Kreis der bedeutendsten in der Schweiz vor dem Ersten Weltkrieg realisierten Hotelbauten. Es repräsentiert den Höhepunkt der Schweizer Hotellerie in der Belle Époque sowohl in bautechnischer als auch in gestalterischer Hinsicht. Die Bau- und Gebäudetechnik sowie der Fassadenschmuck gehörten zum Fortschrittlichsten ihrer Zeit.

Blick vom Lesesaal ins Vestibül, 1906
View from the reading room to the vestibule, 1906

1   Luzerner Tagblatt, 9. Mai 1906, S. 1.
2   Luzerner Tages-Anzeiger, 9. Mai 1906, S. 2.
3   Dieser Text basiert, wo nicht anders vermerkt, auf: Peter Omachen, Luzern – eine Touristenstadt. Hotelarchitektur von 1782 bis 1914, Baden 2010.
4   Jochen Hesse, «Meili-Wapf, Heinrich», in: Isabelle Rucki und Dorothee Huber (Hg.), Architektenlexikon der Schweiz: 19./20. Jahrhundert, Basel Boston Berlin 1998, S. 368f.
5   Roland Sigrist, «Franz Josef Bucher», in: Historisches Lexikon der Schweiz (HLS) https://hls-dhs-dss.ch/de/articles/030309/2004-06-08/ (zuletzt abgerufen: 13.08.2022).

typical canopy known as the Welscher Haube, two side avant-corps, a heightened base level with solid ashlar bossage masonry, three hierarchically structured guest-room floors and a mansard-roof conclusion. However, details show numerous deviations from the traditional formal canon. They begin with the floor plan, with no symmetry between the two side avant-corps. The façade and roof design also has clearly contrasting lakeside corners. The gable, the dome-like roof and the tower effectively loosen up the silhouette, while the townside corner tower also gives the Palace its unmistakeable appearance.

Meili-Wapf uses traditional elements for the façades, such as wall pilasters in the avant-corps, as well as pilaster strips and capitals. By contrast, the actual décor with its floral forms reveals art nouveau influences. The numerous sculptural works on the façade were produced by the renowned artists Hugo Siegwart and Joseph Zbinden.

APPRECIATION

Visible from afar, the Hotel Palace is a dominant feature of Lucerne's quay promenade. Together with the Hotel National further towards the city centre and the Kursaal situated between the two hotels, it forms part of a striking triad of prominent tourist buildings on Lucerne's lake basin. The building is surrounded by additional former and still existent hotels from the Belle Époque period. However, all of these are situated on the slope side of Haldenstrasse, running parallel to the lake.

The Palace is one of the most important Swiss hotel buildings constructed before World War I. It represents the climax of the Swiss hotel sector during the Belle Époque, both in terms of structural engineering and with respect to its design. The building method and the technical systems it used, as well as its façade ornamentation, were among the most modern of its time.

1   *Luzerner Tagblatt*, May 9, 1906, p. 1.
2   *Luzerner Tages-Anzeiger*, May 9, 1906, p. 2.
3   Unless noted otherwise, this text is based on: Peter Omachen, *Luzern – eine Touristenstadt. Hotelarchitektur von 1782 bis 1914*, Baden 2010.
4   Jochen Hesse, "Meili-Wapf, Heinrich", in: Isabelle Rucki and Dorothee Huber (Eds.), *Architektenlexikon der Schweiz: 19./20. Jahrhundert*, Basel Boston Berlin 1998, p. 368f.
5   Roland Sigrist, "Franz Josef Bucher", in: *Historisches Lexikon der Schweiz* (HLS) https://hls-dhs-dss.ch/de/articles/030309/2004-06-08/ (last accessed: 13.08.2022).

Das Hotel Palace mit dem Hotel National im Vordergrund, dahinter der Kursaal vor seinem Umbau 1912. Foto um 1906
The Hotel Palace with the Hotel National in the foreground and the Kursaal in between, before its conversion in 1912. Photo taken in 1906

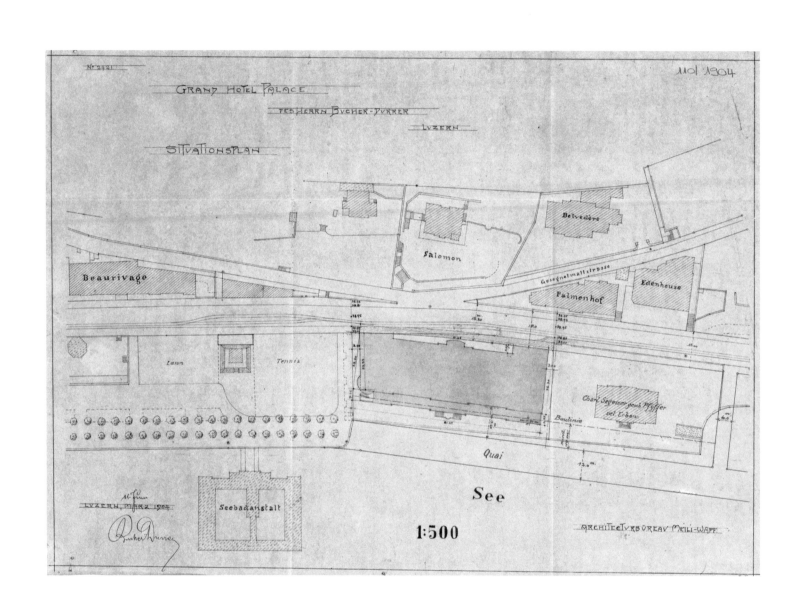

Seiten 34–43: Ausführungspläne, Heinrich Meili-Wapf, 1906
Pages 34–43: Pre-construction drawings, Heinrich Meili-Wapf, 1906

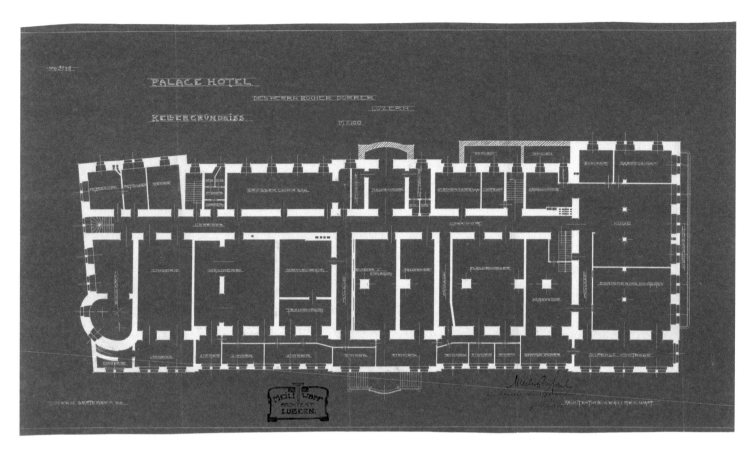

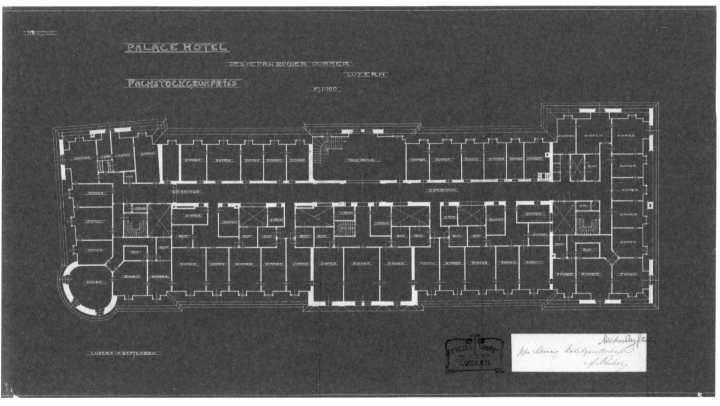

PALACE HOTEL

DES HERRN BUCHER DURRER

WESTFAÇADE   LUZERN   OSTFAÇADE

M 1:100

LUZERN SEPTEMBER 04

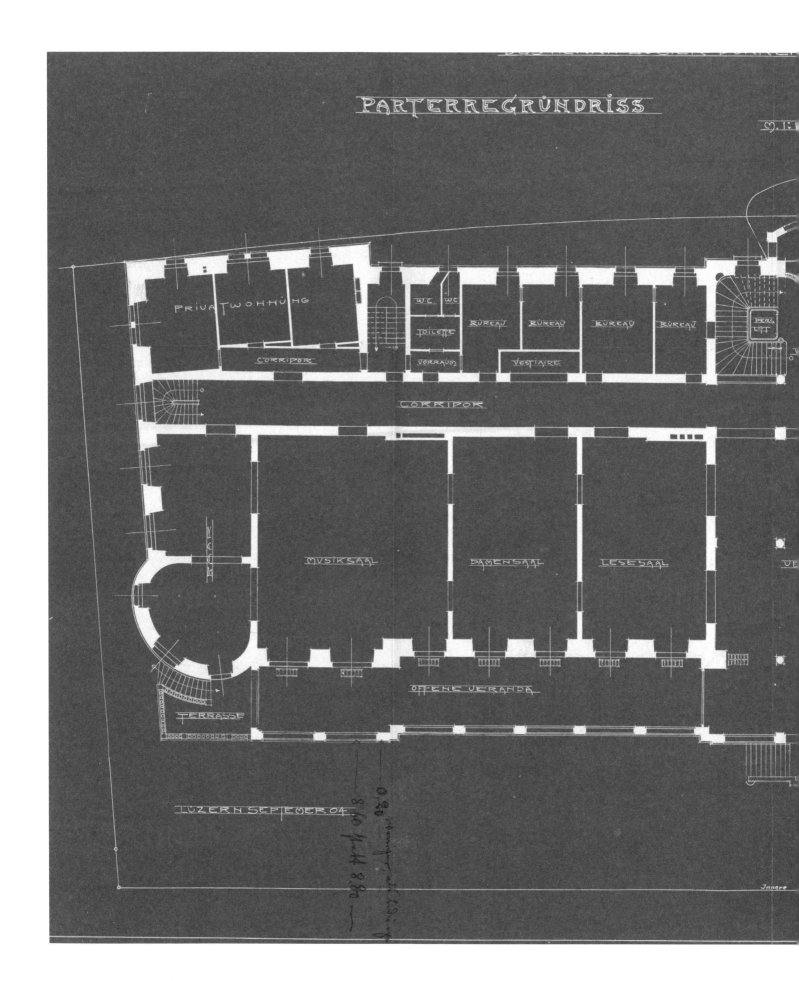

PARTERREGRÜNDRISS

M. 1:

PRIVATWOHNUNG

CORRIDOR

W.C WC

TOILETTE

VORRAUM

BUREAU BUREAU BUREAU BUREAU

VESTIAIRE

PERS LIFT

CORRIDOR

MUSIKSAAL

DAMENSAAL

LESESAAL

VE

OFFENE VERANDA

TERRASSE

LUZERN SEPTEMBER 04

Jenger

38

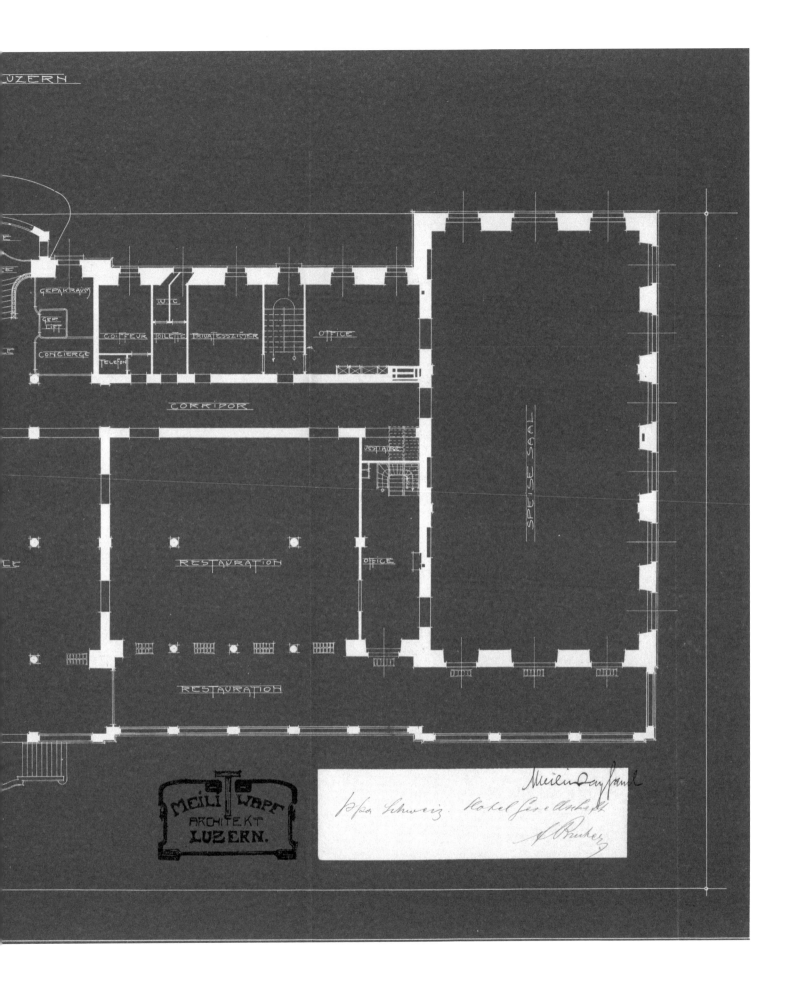

LUZERN

GEPÄKRAUM
GEP LIFT
CONCIERGE
COIFFEUR
TOILETTE
PRIVATESSZIMER
W.C.
OFFICE
TELEFON
CORRIDOR
SPEISE SAAL
RESTAURATION
OFFICE
RESTAURATION

MEILI WAPF
ARCHITEKT
LUZERN.

PALACE HOTEL

DES HERRN RUGER-DURR

I. STOCKGRUNDRISS

M 1:100

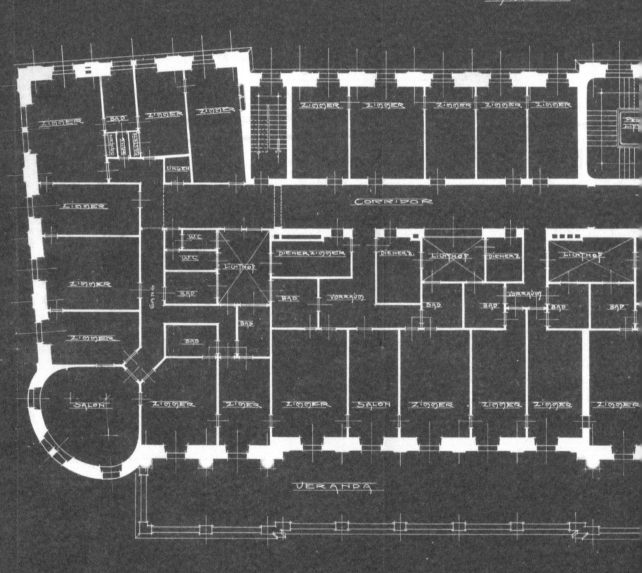

LUZERN, SEPTEMBER 04

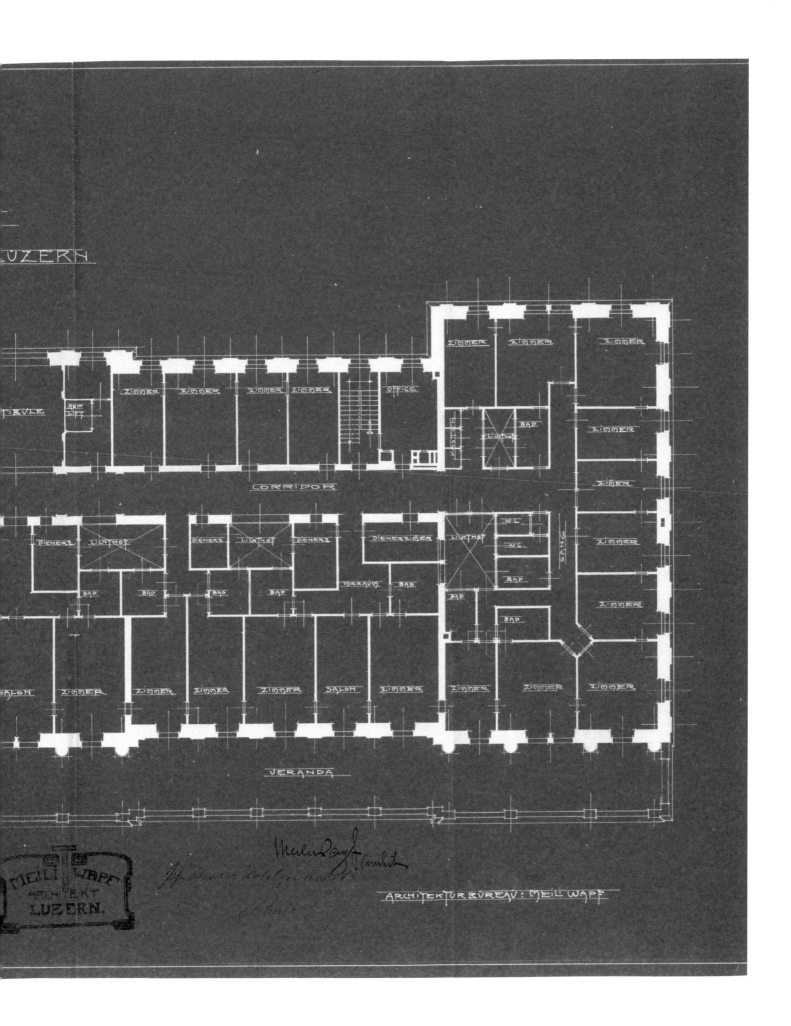

LUZERN

ZIMMER ZIMMER ZIMMER ZIMMER OFFICE ZIMMER ZIMMER ZIMMER

VESTIBULE LIFT

ZIMMER

CORRIDOR

LICHTHOF BAD

ZIMMER

DIENERZ LICHTHOF DIENERZ LICHTHOF DIENERZ DIENERZIMMER LICHTHOF

BAD BAD BAD BAD VORRAUM BAD W.C.

W.C.

BAD ZIMMER

BAD

ZIMMER ZIMMER ZIMMER ZIMMER ZIMMER SALON ZIMMER ZIMMER ZIMMER ZIMMER

SALON ZIMMER GANG

VERANDA

ARCHITEKTURBUREAU : MEILI WAPF

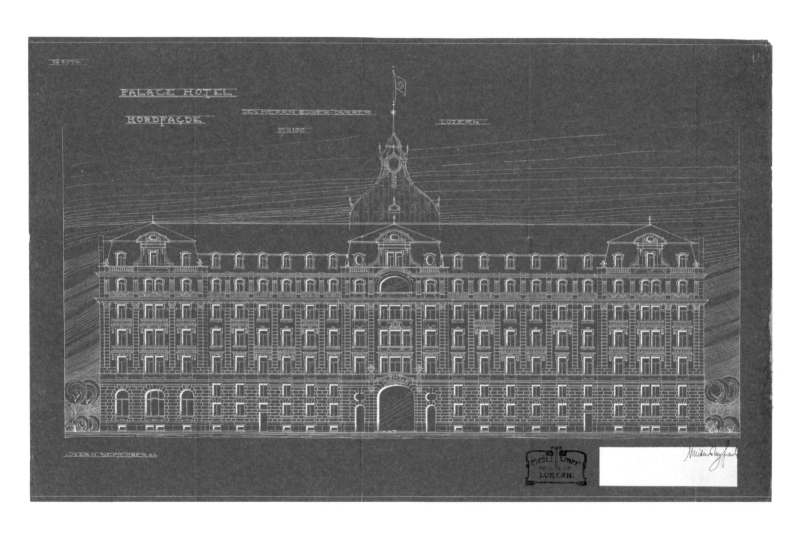

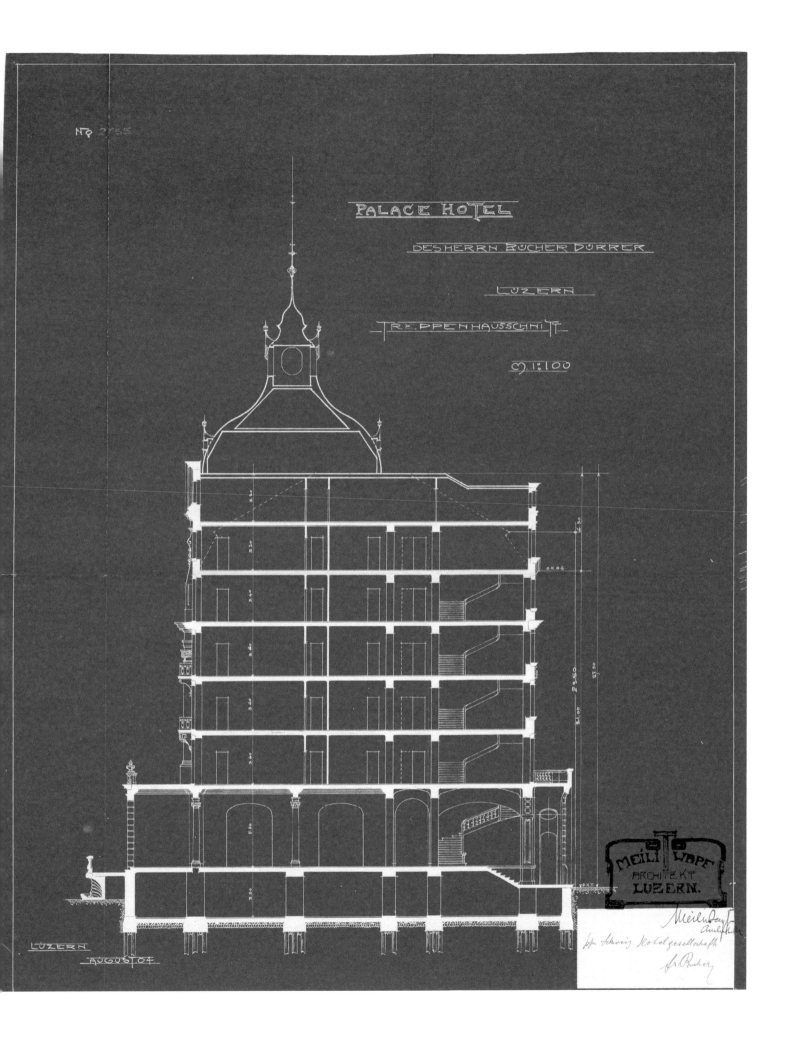

PALACE HOTEL

DES HERRN BUCHER DURRER

LUZERN

TREPPENHAUSSCHNITT

M. 1:100

No 2755

LUZERN
AUGUST 04

MEILI WAPF
ARCHITEKT
LUZERN.

WICHTIGE UMBAUTEN UND VERÄNDERUNGEN
BIS 2016

Iwan Bühler

DIE HALDENSTRASSE

Die Haldenstrasse war zur Zeit der Erbauung des Hotel Palace eine Nebenstrasse, welche den Autofahrer dem See entlang nach Küssnacht am Rigi über die Axenstrasse nach Flüelen und dann über den Gotthard ins Tessin führte. Es gab auch eine einspurige Tramverbindung, die vor dem Hotel Palace vorbeifuhr.

Das Verkehrsaufkommen war damals noch sehr gering, weshalb der Haupteingang ins Hotel im Bereich des Mittelrisalits an der Haldenstrasse lag. Kutschen, vereinzelt Autos und die Tram fuhren direkt zum Eingang. Nach der Begrüssung der Gäste wurden die Fahrzeuge vom Personal entladen und stadtauswärts an der Strasse parkiert.

Der Empfang im Hotelvestibül war für den Gast ein besonderes Erlebnis: Die lichtdurchflutete Hotelhalle mit ihren quadratischen Bodenplatten aus Marmor, den grünlichen Wandbelägen, dazu die opulenten Stuckdecken mit den grossen Kronleuchtern müssen eine beeindruckende Wirkung auf die Ankommenden gehabt haben. Nicht zu vergessen, der Ausblick auf See und Berge.

Der individuelle Autoverkehr nahm über die Jahre stetig zu, im Jahr 1965 wurde die Haldenstrasse von einer Nebenstrasse zu einer Hauptstrasse innerorts erklärt. Auch das Reisen mit Bussen wurde attraktiver, was den Hotelbetrieb vor eine immer grössere Herausforderung stellte. Die Busgäste mit ihren Koffern mussten bei ihrer Ankunft sicher ins Hotel gebracht werden. Das nahm viel Zeit in Anspruch, dazu kam der im Privatauto Reisende, der auch adäquat empfangen werden wollte, obwohl die Platzverhältnisse vor dem Hoteleingang beschränkt waren. Das alles führte zu Behinderungen des Verkehrsflusses an der Haldenstrasse und zu immer mehr Beschwerden aus der Luzerner Stadtbevölkerung.

Im Jahr 1957 wurden die hoteleigenen Tennisplätze aufgrund dieser Platznot in einen öffentlichen Parkplatz mit 50 Autoabstellplätzen zwischen dem Hotel Casino/Kursaal und dem Palace umgenutzt.

Das Verkehrsaufkommen nahm in den folgenden Jahren weiterhin rasant zu, daher musste nach weiteren Parkflächen gesucht werden.

Als 1998 ein unterirdisches Parkhaus mit sechs oberirdischen Carparkplätzen anstelle des oberirdischen Parkplatzes gebaut wurde, wurde der Hoteleingang an die Westseite des Hauses verlegt, was zu der geforderten Entspannung entlang der Haldenstrasse führte, dafür aber zu neuen Problemen innerhalb der vorhandenen Hotelstruktur.

Tram an der Haldenstrasse, 1929
Tram along Haldenstrasse in 1929

Postkarte, 1906
Postcard, 1906

IMPORTANT CONVERSIONS AND CHANGES BEFORE 2016

Iwan Bühler

HALDENSTRASSE

When the Hotel Palace was built, Haldenstrasse was a side street used by cars to drive along the lake shore towards Küssnacht am Rigi, before continuing further along Axenstrasse to Flüelen and on to Ticino via the Gotthard pass. A single-track tram line used to run past the Hotel Palace.

At the time, traffic levels were very limited, which is why the main entrance was still situated at the central avant-corps facing Haldenstrasse. Coaches, occasional cars and the tram led directly to the entrance. After welcoming the guests, staff unloaded the vehicles and parked them along the street further out of town.

The reception in the hotel vestibule was a special experience for guests: flooded with light, the hotel hall with its square marble floor slabs, greenish wall surfaces and opulent stucco ceilings with large chandeliers must have made a lasting impression on the new arrivals. Not to mention the view of the lake and mountains.

Over the decades, car volumes steadily increased and in 1965, Haldenstrasse's official status as a side street was changed to an inner-urban main road. Travel with buses also became more attractive, posing ever greater challenges to hotel operations. Guests arriving by bus had to be chaperoned and their suitcases carried inside. That took a great deal of time, in addition to guests arriving in their private cars. They also wanted to be received adequately, although space at the hotel entrance was limited. This all led to bottlenecks on Haldenstrasse and an increasing number of complaints from Lucerne's residents.

In 1957, in response to the constricted space, the hotel's own tennis courts were converted into a public car park for 50 vehicles between the hotel casino/Kursaal and the Palace.

In the following years, traffic volumes continued to increase rapidly, making it necessary to seek additional parking spaces.

In 1998, when an underground car park with six above-ground parking spaces was built to replace the existing car park, the hotel entrance was moved to the west side of the building, which relieved the congestion on Haldenstrasse as desired, but also created new problems within the existing hotel structure.

Westfassade und Parkplatz, 1957
West façade and car park, 1957

NEUER HAUPTEINGANG

Als Betonung des «neuen» Haupteingangs an der Stirnseite wurde im Jahr 2005 ein grosses Vordach errichtet, das jedoch trotz aller Bemühungen des Hotelbetreibers nicht darüber hinwegtäuschen kann, dass der Hoteleingang unglücklich positioniert ist. Aus Kostengründen wurde unsere Idee leider gestrichen, das bestehende, von Ingenieuren geplante Vordach zu ersetzen, obwohl es als Auftakt zum Betreten des Gebäudes wichtig wäre, mit einem adäquaten Vordach den Eingang zu markieren. Über einen Windfang im Gebäudeinnern angekommen, wird einem die effektive Länge des Gebäudes bewusst, befindet man sich doch am Anfang des Korridors, der sich durchs ganze Gebäude erstreckt. Der schmale, hohe Gang mit Tonnengewölbe führt den Gast auf direktem Weg an anonymen Türen links und rechts vorbei zum ehemaligen Haupteingang. Zur Rechten öffnet sich die Hotelhalle und gibt den Blick auf See und Berge frei.

Haupteingang West mit Vordach aus dem Jahr 2005
Main entrance, west side, with canopy built in 2005

An dieser kurzen Wegbeschreibung lässt sich das Dilemma ablesen: Der Gast wird lieblos und unmissverständlich ins Zentrum des Hotels geleitet, wo sich dann endlich die Rezeption findet – eine Situation, die nicht auf das Grand Hotel am See schliessen lässt.

EINGANGSHALLE, KORRIDOR

Ursprünglich betrat der Gast durch eine elegante Drehtür das weitläufige, repräsentative Vestibül. Die grossen Bogenöffnungen gaben den Blick durch die lichtdurchflutete Halle direkt auf den See, die Stadt und die Berge frei. Die Ankunft war eine Inszenierung und spielte mit der exklusiven Grosszügigkeit der Räume sowie der atemberaubenden Umgebung Luzerns.

Die Halle mit ihren roten Säulen, den quadratischen Bodenplatten aus Marmor, den grünlich-rosafarbigen Wandbelägen aus Stuckmarmor und den opulenten Stuckdecken mit grossen Kronleuchtern vermittelte einen ebenso luxuriösen Eindruck wie der umlaufende Horizont aus Stuck, der den Raum noch höher erscheinen ließ.

Vestibule/Halle, Fotografie coloriert, 1906
Vestibule, hall, coloured photograph, 1906

Im Vestibül waren der Rezeptionstresen und die Haupttreppe, der Gast wurde beim Eintreten direkt in Empfang genommen. Es ist auch heute noch der perfekte Ort, um eine Hotelführung zu beginnen. Hier wird die schlüssige räumliche Organisation des Gebäudes am deutlichsten sichtbar: Geradeaus ist die Halle mit Terrasse und dem schönen Seeblick. Links und rechts davon befinden sich seeseitig das Restaurant sowie die Salons mit vorgelagerter Veranda, die zum Verweilen einladen. An einem Ende des Korridors der grosse Speisesaal, am anderen der Musiksaal mit Bar. Die nordseitigen Räume dienten überwiegend der Infrastruktur. Die Haupttreppe führte die Gäste zu ihren Zimmern, welche sich beidseitig entlang der Korridore aufreihten.

Der verlegte Haupteingang erforderte, dass die Gäste zur Rezeption begleitet werden mussten. Viele der einst grosszügigen Bogenöffnungen, durch die Licht in den Korridor gelangte, sind mittlerweile verkleinert oder gar ganz geschlossen worden.

Die opulenten Stuckaturen sind im Laufe der Jahre einer Reihe von Modernisierungen zum Opfer gefallen. Das Erlebnis des Ankommens war also viel bescheidener geworden und das Hotel hat im Zuge der vielen Modernisierungen im Laufe des Jahrhunderts einen Grossteil seines historischen Charmes eingebüsst.

NEW MAIN ENTRANCE

In 2005, to highlight the "new" main entrance at the head end, a large canopy was constructed, which however, despite all the efforts of the hotel operator, could not conceal the fact that the entrance's position was less than ideal. Unfortunately, our idea of replacing the canopy, which had been designed by engineers, was rejected on grounds of cost, even though it was important to mark the entrance with an adequate canopy. Visitors enter via a porch and are presented with a view through the entire length of the building, since they are standing at the beginning of the corridor stretching through the volume. The narrow, tall, barrel-vaulted walkway leads visitors directly past anonymous doors to the left and right and also past the former main entrance. The hotel hall opens to the right, revealing a view of the lake and the mountains.

This brief description of their route demonstrates the dilemma: visitors are unceremoniously and unambiguously guided to the centre of the hotel, where they finally find the reception area. Such a situation is not conducive to the idea of being in a lakeside grand hotel.

ENTRANCE HALL, CORRIDOR

Originally, visitors entered the building via an elegant revolving door, stepping into a spacious and prestigious vestibule. The large arched openings presented a view of the lake, the city and the mountains beyond the light-filled hall. Arriving at the hotel was therefore a staged event, playing on the exclusivity of the generous spaces and Lucerne's breath-taking surroundings.

The hall with its red columns, the square marble floor slabs, the greenish and pink scagliola wall coverings and the opulent stucco ceilings with large chandeliers are as impressively luxurious as the surrounding stucco horizon, which makes the room appear even taller.

The reception counters and main stairs were situated directly in the vestibule, allowing visitors to be welcomed immediately as they entered. Even today, it is the perfect place to begin a tour of the hotel, since it makes the hotel's coherent spatial organisation most clearly visible: straight ahead, the hall and patio with its beautiful view of the lake; to the left and right, the lakeside restaurant and the salons with verandas in front of them, inviting visitors to linger. The large dining room is at one end of the corridor, while the music hall and bar are situated at the opposite end. Rooms on the north side were mainly used for infrastructural purposes. The main stairs led hotel guests to their rooms, which were organised on both sides of the corridor.

Repositioning the main entrance meant that visitors had to be guided to the reception. Many of the once spacious apertures, through which a wealth of natural light shone into the building, have by now been downsized or completely closed.

Over the years, the opulent stucco designs have fallen victim to a series of modernising measures. The experience of arrival has therefore become much more modest and the hotel has lost much of its historical charm through the many modernisations over the course of the century.

Konzept neues Vordach, Iwan Bühler Architekten, 2017
Concept for the new covered entrance, Iwan Bühler Architekten, 2017

Eingangshalle, 1980
Entrance hall, 1980

DAS HOTEL IM WANDEL DER ZEIT

Nachdem das Palace nach nur zehn Jahren aufgrund ausbleibender Gäste – der Erste Weltkrieg unterbrach den Touristenstrom abrupt – seine Türen wieder schliessen musste, wurde es von der Schweizer Armee vorübergehend als Reifenlager genutzt. Nach Kriegsende nahm das Haus den Betrieb wieder auf und erlebte in den Zwanzigerjahren erneut eine Blütezeit als gesellschaftlicher Treffpunkt eines eleganten internationalen Publikums.

Die Weltwirtschaftskrise im Jahre 1929 stoppte den wirtschaftlichen Erfolg von Neuem, die drückenden Zinsbelastungen trafen die Besitzer schwer. Dazu kam der Zweite Weltkrieg, das Hotel musste wieder schliessen. Dieses Mal wurde es als Sanitätsanstalt und Vorratslager für die Soldaten genutzt.

Die Bilder aus dieser Zeit zeigen, dass die grossen Säle von der Schweizer Armee im Erdgeschoss als Schlafsäle respektive als Aufenthaltsräume genutzt wurden. Nach Kriegsende wurde das Hotel nach einer zweijährigen Renovierungsphase mit Kosten in der Höhe von 1,5 Mio. Franken wiedereröffnet.

Nebst dem Einbau einer zusätzlichen Bar wurde das Erdgeschoss von zu «üppigem» Zierrat an Decken und Wänden befreit. «Wer modern sein will, muss sich modern zeigen.» Die Gipsornamente an den Stuckdecken wurden entfernt, die Marmorleibungen der Bogentüren abgenommen, die zum See hin orientierten Fenster durch neue, schnörkellose Verglasungen ersetzt, sämtliche Zimmer modernisiert. Einzig der Damensaal blieb im Urzustand als historischer Saal erhalten.

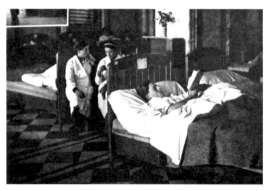

Das Hotel Palace von der Schweizer Armee zu Schlafsälen und Aufenthaltsräumen umgenutzt, Bilder aus einem Zeitungsartikel von 1940
The Swiss Army converted the Hotel Palace into dormatories and common rooms. Photos in a newspaper article, 1940

THE HOTEL THROUGH CHANGING TIMES

Only ten years after it opened, the Palace was forced to close due to a lack of guests: World War I abruptly put an end to the flow of tourists. Instead, it was temporarily used by the Swiss Army as a tyre warehouse. Following the end of the war, the hotel reopened and enjoyed another boom period in the Twenties, serving as a society meeting place for an elegant, international clientele.

The global economic crisis in 1929 brought an end to the hotel's success, as crippling interest rates were a heavy burden on the hotel's owner. Then came World War II, forcing the hotel to close again. This time, it was used as a hospital and warehouse for soldiers.

Images from this period show that the Swiss Army used the large ground-floor salons as dormitory spaces and common rooms. When the war ended, the hotel was again reopened following a two-year period of renovation, costing 1.5 million Francs.

Aside from installing an additional bar, the ground floor saw all of its "ornate" decoration removed from the ceilings and walls. "If you want to modernise, you must be seen to be modern." The plaster ornaments on the stucco ceilings were removed, the marble reveals on the arched doors were dismantled, the windows facing the lake were replaced by new, undecorated glazing, and all rooms were modernised. Only the ladies' salon remained in its original condition as a historical room.

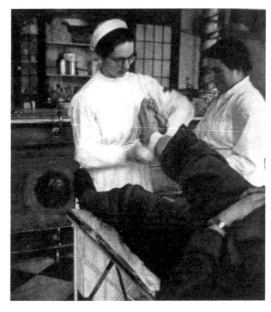

NEUBAU DES ZWEISTUFIGEN MANSARDENDACHES
(5. UND 6. OBERGESCHOSS)

Die in den 1990er-Jahren gute Auslastung des Hotels bewog die Bauherrschaft dazu, die beiden Dachgeschosse komplett neu zu errichten. Die vorhandenen Zimmer konnten den Hotelgästen nicht zugemutet werden, war die Zimmertemperatur doch im Winter zu kalt und im Sommer zu heiss, weshalb sie bis zum Zeitpunkt des Abbruchs nur als Abstellräume genutzt wurden.

Unter der Leitung des damaligen Hoteldirektors Jürg Reinshagen wurde deshalb entschieden, die beiden Dachgeschosse bis auf den Boden des fünften Obergeschosses abzutragen und neu zu errichten. Die beiden vorhandenen Türme sowie die sieben Ziergewände mussten aus denkmalpflegerischen Gründen entgegen dem Wunsch des Auftraggebers bestehen bleiben. Der Umbau fand zwischen November 1993 und Juli 1994 bei laufendem Hotelbetrieb statt.

Einzig das vierte Obergeschoss wurde zeitweise geschlossen, weil mit einem Baugerüst gearbeitet wurde, welches auf dem Balkonsims dieses Geschosses abgestützt wurde, was manchmal zu Immissionen führte. Diese Gerüstvariante wurde gewählt, um von den Zimmern der vier darunterliegenden Geschosse aus weiterhin freie Sicht auf See und Berge zu haben.

Ein wichtiger Aspekt beim Dachneubau war, dass man nicht mehr Gewicht einbringen durfte als abgebaut wurde, denn das Fundament des Hotels besteht aus Eichenpfählen, was für ein Gebäude am See nicht optimal ist. Deshalb kam eine Stahlskelettkonstruktion zum Einsatz. Auf ein Notdach verzichtete man, oberhalb des fünften Obergeschosses wurde jedoch ein wasserdichter Not-Boden aufgebaut. Das sechste Obergeschoss bekam aufgrund des niedrigeren Gewichts einen Elementboden aus Porenbeton. Wegen des engen Umbauzeitrahmens arbeitete man so weit wie möglich mit vorfabrizierten Bauteilen. Die Badezimmer waren, ähnlich wie in Flugzeugen, fertige Kunststoffboxen, die neuen Dachlukarnen wurden bereits in der Werkstatt zusammengebaut und auch das Stahlskelett teilweise vorgefertigt. Diese Massnahmen ermöglichten es, das Hotel in kaum mehr als vier Monaten mit 48 zusätzlichen klimatisierten Zimmern zu erweitern.

Neubau Mansardendach, 1993/94
Newly constructed mansard roof, 1993/94

NEW CONSTRUCTION OF THE TWO-STAGE MANSARD ROOF
(5TH AND 6TH FLOORS)

The hotel's good occupancy levels in the 1990s motivated its owners to completely redesign the top two floors. The existing rooms could not be offered to hotel guests, since they were too cold in the winter and too hot in the summer, which is why they had been used for storage until their demolition.

Under the auspices of the hotel director of the time, Jürg Reinshagen, it was therefore decided to remove the two top floors and rebuild them. The two existing towers and the seven ornamental covers had to be preserved for heritage reasons, against the wishes of the client. The conversion measures were carried out between November 1993 and July 1994, during running hotel operations.

Only the fourth floor was closed for some time, while work was carried out using scaffolding that rested on balcony ledges, thereby occasionally causing emissions. This form of scaffolding was chosen to ensure that the four floors below would continue to enjoy an unobstructed view of the lake and the mountains.

One important aspect of the new roof structure was that it could not be a greater load than the dismantled older roof, since the hotel foundations consisted of oak piles, which is not ideal for structures by a lake. Thus, the new roof was built as a steel skeleton structure. A temporary roof was not used, but a waterproof temporary ceiling was installed above the fifth floor. Due to its low weight, the sixth floor received a weatherproof ceiling made of acerated concrete. In view of the short conversion period, prefabricated building elements were used as much as possible. The bathrooms were inserted as finished artificial boxes in a process similar to aviation construction. The new roof lucarnes were assembled at the workshop and even the steel skeleton was partially prefabricated. These measures made it possible to extend the hotel with 48 additional, air-conditioned rooms in hardly more than four months.

EHEMALIGER MUSIKSAAL

Nach dem Zweiten Weltkrieg wurde ein Seiteneingang in die Westseite des Palace eingebaut, weil man nebst den Hotelgästen auch die Luzerner Bevölkerung im Hotel bewirten und unterhalten wollte. An der Stelle des ehemaligen Musiksaals wurden ein kleines Restaurant, «Le Mignon Grill», zuerst noch ohne eigene Küche, und eine Tanzbar, das «Dancing Intimo», eingerichtet. Schnell wurde das Dancing zum Treffpunkt für ein gehobenes Publikum.

Ganz im damaligen Stil, mit orangefarbenen Wänden, dunkelblauer Decke und gedämpftem Licht hatte der Club gar nichts mehr mit dem luxuriösen Flair der Belle Époque gemeinsam, traf jedoch den Zeitgeist und stärkte den Stellenwert des Hotels. Nach der Schliessung des Dancings durch den damaligen Direktor Jürg Reinshagen konnte das Le Mignon Grill mit Sitzplätzen zum See hin und einer attraktiven Aussenterrasse erweitert werden. Der Erfolg des Restaurants hatte zu diesem Schritt ermutigt, der sich in den folgenden Jahren auch bezahlt machte. 1980 wurde die Terrasse verglast, so konnten die attraktivsten Sitzplätze auch im Winter vergeben werden. Das Restaurant «Marlin», das im Jahr 2003 anstelle des Le Mignon Grill eröffnet wurde, konnte nie an die finanziellen Erfolge seines Vorgängers anknüpfen.

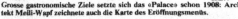

Grosse gastronomische Ziele setzte sich das «Palace» schon 1908: Architekt Meili-Wapf zeichnete auch die Karte des Eröffnungsmenüs.

Ehemaliger Musiksaal, Fotografie coloriert, 1906
Former music hall, coloured, 1906

Ehemaliger Musiksaal, Heinrich Meili-Wapf, 1906
Former music hall, Heinrich Meili-Wapf, 1906

FORMER MUSIC HALL

After World War II, a side entrance was installed on the western side of the Palace, with the aim of catering for and entertaining the residents of Lucerne as well as the hotel guests. The former music hall was converted into a small restaurant, Le Mignon Grill, initially without its own kitchen, and a dance bar, the Dancing Intimo, which quickly became a meeting place for elite society.

Decorated very much in the style of the time, with orange walls, a dark grey ceiling and dim lights, the club no longer had anything to do with the luxurious flair of the Belle Époque, but suited the Zeitgeist and enhanced the hotel's status. After the bar's closure by the director at the time, Jürg Reinshagen, Le Mignon Grill was expanded with seating towards the lake on an attractive patio. The restaurant's success suggested expansion, which paid off in the following years. In 1980, the patio was enclosed by glazing, allowing the most attractive seats to be used all year round. The Marlin, which replaced Le Mignon Grill in 2003, never managed to achieve the same financial success as its predecessor.

Intimo Bar, 1960–1970
Intimo Bar, between 1960 and 1970

Restaurant Minion, 2002
Restaurant Minion, 2002

Restaurant Minion, um 1978
Restaurant Minion, around 1978

Restaurant Marlin, 2016
Restaurant Marlin, 2016

HALLE, BAR

Die Hotelhalle mit ihren vier zentral angeordneten Säulen dient seit der Hoteleröffnung 1906 als Empfangshalle und Treffpunkt für die Hotelgäste. Lichtdurchflutet, übersichtlich, mit visuellem Bezug zum See respektive zur Rezeption und der Haupttreppe, war die Hotelhalle *der* zentrale Raum im Gebäude. Mit sich über die Jahre dem Zeitgeist entsprechend veränderter Bistromöblierung war die Halle der Ort zum Verweilen, Plaudern, Kaffee und Kuchen essen, zum Sehen und Gesehen-Werden.

Mit der Halle durch zwei grosse Rundbogenöffnungen verbunden, befand sich neben dem Damensaal ein Lesesaal mit vorgelagerter, gedeckter Aussenterrasse.

Durch den Einbau der Intimobar musste auch die im Musiksaal angeordnete, etwas versteckte Bar weichen. Der für die Hotelgäste attraktivste Ort war eindeutig der Lesesaal, ideal verbunden mit der Hotelhalle. Deshalb war es nur verständlich, dass hier die neue Bar eingebaut wurde, was den Aufenthalt für den Hotelgast auch am Abend attraktiv machte. Dieser Standort wurde bis zum Umbau beibehalten.

Halle, 1960
Hall, 1960

Halle, 1980
Hall, 1980

Halle, Fotografie coloriert, 1906
Hall, coloured photograph, 1906

HALL, BAR

Since the hotel's opening, the hall, with its four centrally arranged columns, had served as the reception area and meeting place for hotel guests. Brightly illuminated, with plenty of visual references to the lake, the reception area and the main staircase formed the central space of the building. As the bistro furnishing changed with fashions over the years, the hall became a place to gather, chat, enjoy coffee and cake, see and be seen.

Connected to the hall by two large, arched openings, a reading room beside the ladies' salon included a covered outdoor patio in front of it.

The integration of the Intimo Bar made it necessary to remove the somewhat hidden bar in the music hall. The most attractive place for hotel guests was clearly the reading room, with its ideal connection to the hotel hall. Thus, it is understandable that the new bar was installed there, making the location attractive to hotel guests in the evening. The bar remained there until the hotel's conversion.

Halle, 2016
Hall, 2016

Halle, 2002
Hall, 2002

RESTAURANT

Ostseitig befand sich seit je das Restaurant mit Speise- und Festsaal. Im Restaurant, einem wohlproportionierten, ebenfalls zum See hin orientierten Raum mit fünf zentral positionierten tragenden Säulen und einer auf diese abgestimmten Kassettendecke wurden die Gäste kulinarisch verwöhnt. Die Küche befand sich anfangs im Untergeschoss und war durch eine Treppe und einen Speiselift mit dem Restaurantoffice im Erdgeschoss verbunden. Wegen der Zunahme des Touristenstromes nach dem Ende des Zweiten Weltkriegs gelangte die Restaurantinfrastruktur schnell an ihre Grenzen und musste den Bedürfnissen angepasst werden. Der Einbau einer Fertigungsküche auf Erdgeschossniveau wurde unumgänglich, weshalb das Restaurant flächenmässig reduziert werden musste. Aus diesem Grund verschwanden zwei der fünf Säulen in der neu errichteten Küchentrennwand. Damit die Raumsymmetrie optisch im Lot blieb, hat man die drei verbliebenen um eine vierte ergänzt. Der vorhandene, nicht originale Marmorboden wurde belassen, ist er doch farblich gut auf die Stuckmarmorfarbe der Säulen abgestimmt. Auch die vorhandenen, dem Original nachgebauten Kronleuchter verblieben im Restaurant. Um im Garten besser bedienen zu können, erhielt die Küche einen direkten Ausgang im Untergeschoss.

Der Speisesaal wurde im Jahre 1972 zu einem Kongress- und Festsaal umgebaut. Diese Nutzung blieb bis heute erhalten, lediglich die Saaltechnik musste komplett erneuert werden. Durch eine technisch notwendige abgehängte Decke ging die Raumproportion leider verloren.

Restaurant, Heinrich Meili-Wapf, 1906
Restaurant, Heinrich Meili-Wapf, 1906

Restaurant, um 1950
Restaurant around 1950

RESTAURANT

The restaurant, dining room and festive hall have always been situated on the building's east side. Guests were pampered with culinary delights in the restaurant, a well-proportioned space that is also orientated towards the lake, with five centrally positioned load-bearing columns and a coordinated, coffered space. To begin with, the kitchen was situated in the basement and was connected to the restaurant office on the ground floor by stairs and dumb waiter. Due to the increased numbers of tourists after the end of World War II, the restaurant infrastructure was quickly pushed to its limits and had to be adapted to requirements. It was essential to install a kitchen on the ground floor to prepare the meals, which meant reducing the size of the restaurant. Thus, two of the five columns disappeared within the newly constructed kitchen partition wall. To ensure the visual symmetry remained balanced, a further column was added to the three that were still visible. The existing, non-original marble flooring was retained, since it well suited the colour of the scagliola on the columns. The existing chandeliers, copies of the originals, also remained in the restaurant. To improve the service for guests in the garden, the restaurant received a direct exit from the kitchen in the basement.

In 1972, the lake-side dining room was converted into a congress and festive hall and has kept that function to this day. Only the hall's technical systems had to be completely renewed. Unfortunately, the technically required suspended ceiling undermined its spatial proportions.

Restaurant, 2016
Restaurant, 2016

Restaurant im Umbau, Iwan Bühler Architekten, 2021
Nichtragende Säulenergänzung von 2001
Restaurant conversion, Iwan Bühler Architekten, 2021
Free-standing, additional column, 2001

EIN VIERTELJAHRHUNDERT IM HOTEL PALACE

Gespräch zwischen Jürg R. Reinshagen, Direktor und Miteigentümer des Hotels Palace 1971 bis 1997, und Iwan Bühler

Herr Reinshagen, in was für einem Zustand haben Sie das Hotel 1971 übernommen?
Das Hotel war grundsätzlich in gutem Zustand. Man hatte es aber in den Jahren zuvor verabsäumt, die ständig notwendigen Erneuerungen zu tätigen, welche bei einem so grossen Haus jedes Jahr nötig sind.

Was waren denn die ersten Schritte, die Sie unternommen haben, um das Hotel zu modernisieren?
Das Palace war, wie auch andere Hotels, z.B. das Hotel Europe in Luzern, seit der Eröffnung ein reiner Sommerbetrieb. Ab Oktober bis Ostern hatten wir geschlossen. Die Zimmer konnten im Winter nur schlecht geheizt werden. Von 1971 bis 1978 haben wir deshalb über die Wintermonate die Heizung saniert. Die Heizkörper befanden sich an den Innenwänden der jeweiligen Zimmer, die mussten alle an die Aussenwände versetzt werden. Von da an konnten wir das Hotel endlich im Ganzjahresbetrieb geöffnet halten. Es ist unglaublich zeitaufwendig, wenn man das Personal nur über die Saison einstellen kann und jedes Jahr auf's Neue auf ein gutes Team hoffen muss.

Wurde der Haupteingang in Ihrer Zeit als Direktor von der Haldenstrasse an die Westfassade verschoben?
Nein, diese Veränderung kam erst später. Die Hotelgäste sind immer über den Eingang an der Haldenstrasse im Hotel angekommen. Nach dem Zweiten Weltkrieg wurde ein Seiteneingang an der Westfassade eingebaut, weil man ein kleines Restaurant, das Mignon, und die Intimobar, eine Tanzbar für die Luzerner Bevölkerung, einrichten wollte. Die Intimo Bar wurde nach Jahren von mir wieder geschlossen, weil sich eine Klientel breitmachte, die nicht zu unseren Hotelgästen passte. Das Problem war, dass keine räumliche Abtrennung zwischen der Intimo Bar und dem Hotel möglich war. Die nötige Sicherheit war nicht vorhanden. Wir haben die Intimobar deshalb aufgelöst und stattdessen seeseitig das Restaurant eingebaut. Das Mignon blieb dann bis zu meinem Rückzug aus dem Hotelbetrieb bestehen.

Gab es in Ihrer Zeit als Direktor auch Veränderungen in der Hotelküche?
Die Grossküche befand sich immer im Untergeschoss. Das Mignon hatte anfangs keine eigene Küche. Um die Speisen auch dort warm zu servieren, wurde kurz nach der Restauranteröffnung eine Satellitenküche eingebaut. Der grosse Speisesaal wurde im Winter nur geöffnet, wenn es einen Anlass gab.

Das fünfte und sechste Geschoss, die Dachgeschosse – wurden die während Ihrer Zeit als Direktor komplett erneuert?
Ja, das war in den Jahren 1993 bis 1994. Diese Zimmer konnten kaum vermietet werden. Im Sommer waren sie viel zu heiss, im Winter hat man gefroren. Sie waren unbrauchbar. Deshalb haben wir diese zwei Geschosse komplett zurückgebaut und mittels Stahlbaus wieder aufgebaut. Es musste eine Leichtbaukonstruktion sein, steht doch das Palace am Seeufer, ist suboptimal gepfählt und darf nicht mit zusätzlichem Gewicht belastet werden.

Hatte das Hotel eigene Abstellplätze für die Autos der Gäste?
Die Autos wurden vor dem Haupteingang vom Personal übernommen, entladen und dann in der Verlängerung an der Haldenstrasse parkiert. Auf dem Gelände vor dem Hotel, zwischen Casino und Palace, da wo sich früher die hoteleigenen Tennisplätze befunden hatten, gab es weitere Parkmöglichkeiten.

A QUARTER OF A CENTURY AT THE HOTEL PALACE

A conversation between Jürg R. Reinshagen, Director and Co-owner of the Hotel Palace from 1971 to 1997, and Iwan Bühler

Jürg Reinshagen, what was the hotel's condition when you took over as Director in 1971?
The hotel was fundamentally in good shape. However, in the years before, regular, essential renovation measures had been neglected. These are required every year because the building is so large.

What were the first steps you took to modernise the hotel?
Like other hotels, such as the Hotel Europe in Lucerne, the Palace had always exclusively been a summer hotel. It remained closed from October to Easter. The rooms were difficult to heat in the winter. So from 1971 to 1978, we refurbished the heating system during the winter months. The radiators were situated on the inner walls of the rooms and they all had to be moved to the outer walls. From then on, the hotel could finally open all year round. It is incredibly work-intensive if you can only employ the staff during the season and then have to hope for a good team the following year.

Was the main entrance moved from Haldenstrasse to the western façade while you were the hotel Director?
No, that change only happened later. The hotel guests always used the Haldenstrasse entrance to get into the building. After World War II, a side entrance on the western façade was installed with the aim of establishing a small restaurant, the Mignon, and the Intimobar, a dance bar for Lucerners. A few years later, I closed the Intimobar because its regular clientele didn't suit our hotel guests. The problem was that it was impossible to partition the Intimo Bar and the hotel. There was not enough security. Thus we closed the Intimo Bar and established the restaurant on the lake side instead. The Mignon continued to exist until I withdrew from the hotel business.

During your time as Director, were there any changes to the hotel kitchen?
The large kitchen has always been situated in the basement. To begin with, the Mignon had no kitchen of its own, so to ensure that dishes were served warm, a satellite kitchen was installed shortly after the restaurant opened. The large dining room was only opened in winter on special occasions.

Were the fifth and sixth floors, the attic levels, completely refurbished during your period as Director?
Yes, that was from 1993 to 1994. The rooms could hardly be booked. In the summer they were much too hot, while in winter they were freezing, making them unusable. So we completely dismantled those two floors and rebuilt them using steel structures. It had to be a lightweight structure since the Palace is situated by a lake, does not have ideal pile foundations and cannot support additional weight.

Did the hotel have its own parking spaces for guests?
The cars were received by our staff at the main entrance, unloaded and then parked along the Haldenstrasse extension. Additional parking spaces were available on the grounds in front of the hotel, between the Casino and the Palace, where the hotel's own tennis courts had originally existed.

How important was the music festival for Lucerne's hotel sector?
When I became Director at the Palace, the hotel managers did virtually nothing for the music festival. The hotel industry and the public hardly took notice of the annual international event. My father was a conductor and I grew up with classical music. In 1971, back in Lucerne, I took every opportunity to attend a classical concert. In this way, I developed contacts with conductors and musicians, so naturally I took care of them.

Wie wichtig waren die Musikfestwochen für die Luzerner Hotellerie?
Als ich das Direktorenamt im Palace übernommen habe, haben sich die Hoteliers kaum um die Musikfestwochen bemüht. Von diesem jährlichen internationalen Ereignis hat die Hotellerie und die Bevölkerung kaum Notiz genommen. Mein Vater war Dirigent, ich bin mit klassischer Musik aufgewachsen und 1971, zurück in Luzern, habe ich jede Gelegenheit wahrgenommen, ein klassisches Konzert zu besuchen. Auf diese Weise bin ich in Kontakt mit den Dirigenten und den Musikern gekommen und habe mich selbstverständlich um sie gekümmert.

Wer ging damals im Hotel ein und aus?
Herbert von Karajan, Leonard Bernstein, Artur Rubinstein, um nur einige zu nennen. Mit dem einen oder anderen habe ich über die Jahre richtig Freundschaft geschlossen. Leider haben es die Käufer des Hotels 1997 verpasst, diese Kontakte weiterzupflegen. Ich hoffe sehr, dass das Palace wieder an frühere Zeiten anknüpfen kann, Luzern als Touristenstadt braucht ein erfolgreiches Fünfsternehaus.

Lieber Herr Reinshagen, ich danke Ihnen für das Gespräch.
Luzern, 10. Mai 2022

Jürg Reinshagen mit Pianist Artur Rubinstein (1887–1982)
Jürg Reinshagen with the pianist Artur Rubenstein (1887–1982)

Jürg Reinshagen mit Walter Scheel Bundespräsident der Bundesrepublik Deutschland 1974–1979
Jürg Reinshagen with Walter Scheel, President of the Federal Republic of Germany, 1974–1979

Which famous people frequented the hotel back then?
Herbert von Karajan, Leonard Bernstein and Artur Rubinstein, to name just a few. I developed a true friendship with some of them over the years. Unfortunately, when the hotel was sold in 1997, the new owners failed to maintain those contacts. I truly hope the Palace can regain the status it enjoyed in former, happier times. The tourist city of Lucerne needs a successful five-star establishment.

Thank you for talking to us!
Lucerne, May 10, 2022

Jürg Reinshagen mit Mariss Jansons (lettischer Dirigent, 1943–2019) und seiner Frau Irina
Jürg Reinshagen with Mariss Jansons (Latvian condutor, 1943–2019) and his wife Irina

Jürg Reinshagen mit Sir James Galway (klassischer Flötist)
Jürg Reinshagen with Sir James Galway (classical flautist)

ARCHITEKTONISCHE ASPEKTE DER ERNEUERUNG

Iwan Bühler

Das Hotel Palace erfuhr seit seiner Errichtung immer wieder bauliche Veränderungen. Diese waren zum Teil grundlegende strukturelle und technische Veränderungen, zum Teil den jeweils aktuellen Bedürfnissen des Gastes geschuldete. Man war die beste Adresse am Vierwaldstättersee und wollte das auch bleiben.

Dass dem Bestand im Rahmen der diversen Umbauten nicht immer die gebührende Wertschätzung entgegengebracht wurde und die getätigten Eingriffe oft nicht überzeugend geplant und umgesetzt waren, ist eine Tatsache, die dem Stellenwert des Hotels als First-Class-Hotel eher geschadet hat.

Was ist nun zu tun, wie können die Vorstellungen des Bauherrn zu seiner Zufriedenheit umgesetzt, wie kann dem Gebäude die Bedeutung zurückgegeben werden, die es verdient? Das waren die Fragen, die ich mir mit meinen Mitarbeitern und Mitarbeiterinnen gestellt habe. Nach intensivem Studium des vorhandenen Quellenmaterials – Originalpläne, Fotos vom Bau, verschiedene zeitgenössische Texte – hatten wir uns ein fundiertes Bild vom Urzustand erarbeitet, das uns erlaubte, die verschiedenen bisherigen Veränderungen zu analysieren, einzuordnen und zu bewerten und aus diesem Wissen heraus das Umbaukonzept zu entwickeln.

In Zusammenarbeit mit der Denkmalpflege legten wir uns darauf fest, die noch vorhandenen Elemente des bauzeitlichen Zustands des Hotels zu konservieren und gleichzeitig die Vorstellungen der Bauherrschaft so ins Gebäude zu integrieren, dass ein in gestalterischer und bautechnischer Hinsicht zeitgemässes Weiterbauen mit Respekt vor dem Urbestand gewährleistet werden kann. Die architektonischen Eingriffe – das betrifft vor allem das Erdgeschoss, das Treppenhaus und die Erschliessungskorridore in den Obergeschossen – sollten ein qualitätsvolles, vereinheitlichendes und stimmungsvolles Ergebnis erzielen, so dass das Gebäude nach all den Veränderungen der letzten hundert Jahre wieder ein «neues Ganzes» werden kann.

ARCHITECTURAL ASPECTS OF THE REFURBISHMENT

Iwan Bühler

Since its construction, the Hotel Palace has seen repeated structural changes. Some of these were fundamental structural and technical transformations, partly caused by the guests' changing requirements, since the hotel wanted to uphold its status as the best establishment on Lake Lucerne.

Actually, that status was undermined by the fact that some of the many conversion measures failed to appreciate the existing structures and were not convincingly planned or implemented.

My team and I were faced with the questions: what should be done now and how can the client's wishes be implemented satisfactorily, while restoring the building's deserved important status? After intensive study of the existing source materials – original plans, construction photos and various contemporaneous texts – we developed a well-founded picture of the hotel's original condition, allowing us to analyse, classify and assess various changes to date, before using that knowledge to develop a conversion concept.

In collaboration with the monument preservation authority, we determined to preserve the existing elements of the original building fabric, while also integrating the client's wishes into the building to create a contemporary form of continued building on the original structure, both in terms of design and the construction method. The architectural interventions – above all on the ground floor, the stairs and the access corridors on the upper levels – were aimed at achieving a high-quality, unifying and atmospheric result, allowing the hotel to present itself as a "new unity" despite all the changes over the last 100 years.

Aus Architektensicht galt es in dem Sinne korrigierend einzugreifen, dass die räumlichen Qualitäten im Inneren wieder spür- und erlebbar werden, obwohl der ehemalige Haupteingang mit seinen ganzen Raumabfolgen im Erdgeschoss nicht adäquat ersetzt werden konnte. Ohne grössere substanzielle Eingriffe in die Raumstruktur des 2021 unter Denkmalschutz gestellten Hotels war es uns wichtig, dem Gast Orientierung, Geborgenheit und Wohlbefinden zu vermitteln. Nachdem die Aussicht auf See und Berge ein zentrales Charakteristikum des Hotels ist, sollte der tunnelartige Korridor möglichst geöffnet werden, damit die aussergewöhnliche Lage wieder erlebbar wird. Deshalb wurde das ehemalige Marlin im neuen Hotelkonzept zu einem lichtdurchfluteten, zum See hin orientierten Raum umfunktioniert, wo sich nun die grosszügige Rezeption befindet. Die drei Zugangstüren vom Gang sind neu verglast und laden den Hotelgast ein, in der Rezeption zu verweilen. Es gibt genügend Sitzplätze und eine Bibliothek, und die ehemalige, früher als gedeckter Aussensitzplatz genutzte Hotelterrasse, die jetzt ein vorgelagerter Innenraum mit wunderbarer Aussicht ist, kann von jedermann genutzt werden.

Der nun also zur Rezeption umgenutzte Raum – ehemals Musiksaal, dann Intimo Bar, dann Restaurant Merlin – ist jener Raum im Erdgeschoss des Hotels, der die meisten Veränderungen erfahren hat, weshalb weder an Decke noch an Wänden und Boden Originalteile vorhanden sind.

Als Bodenbelag wurde ein farblich zurückhaltender Terrazzoboden gewählt, der sehr gut zu den im Flur bestehenden schwarz-weissen, im Schachbrettmuster verlegten Original Carrara Marmorböden passt. Die Intarsien, mit denen ein Terrazzo normalerweise ergänzt wird, wurden auch hier verwendet. Sie erhielten aber eine neue Dimension, nämlich 11 x 11 Zentimeter, was sich mit dem Grundgedanken deckt, Alt und Neu so zueinander in Beziehung zu setzen, dass eine spannende Wechselwirkung entsteht. (Vgl. das Olivetti Ladenlokal von Carlo Scarpa in Venedig, 1957–1958)

Das optische Integrieren der Rezeption in den Korridor – oder umgekehrt – schafft ganz neue Raumbezüge. Der Rezeption vorgelagert befindet sich die ehemalig gedeckte Aussenterrasse, nebenan gibt es eine neue, zur Stadt und zum See hin orientierte Hausbibliothek. Eine Verbindung zum Damensaal, dem einzigen in seinen Urzustand zurückversetzten, für den Privatgebrauch zur Verfügung stehenden Aufenthalts-, Besprechungs- oder Speisesaal wurde wiederhergestellt.

From the perspective of an architect, it was therefore sensible to apply corrective measures to make the interior spatial qualities more tangible again, even though there was no adequate replacement for the former main entrance and all of its spatial sequences on the ground floor. Without carrying out extreme, substantial interventions to the spatial structure of the hotel, which became preservation-listed in 2021, we found it important to provide guests with a sense of orientation, security and wellbeing. Since the view of the lake and mountains is a key aspect of the hotel's character, the tunnel-like corridor had to be opened as much as possible, in order to experience the exceptional location. Thus, in the new hotel concept, the former Marlin restaurant was transformed into a space suffused with light that faced the lake and accommodated the spacious reception area. The three re-glazed entrance doors invite guests to linger in the reception area. There are enough seats and a library, while the former hotel patio, which had previously been used as a covered outdoor seating area, is now an interior space in front of the salon, which can be used by everyone.

The ground-floor reception area, formerly a music hall, then the Intimo Bar, then the Marlin restaurant, has experienced the most changes of all, which is why neither the ceiling nor the walls have any remaining original elements.

The flooring consists of terrazzo in a reserved tone and harmonises very well with the hallway's black and white original Carrara marble flooring in a chequered design. The inlays that generally accompany terrazzo floors were also used there, although they now have different dimensions of 11 x 11 centimetres, which conform to the underlying concept of establishing a relationship between old and new elements to create exciting interaction (cf. the Olivetti showroom by Carlo Scarpa in Venice, 1957–1958).

The reception area's visual integration into the corridor – and vice versa – creates new spatial references. The formerly covered patio is situated in front of the reception area, while a new hotel library facing the city and lake is situated beside it. A connection to the ladies' salon, the only room that was restored to its original condition, was re-established; it fulfils private functions as a venue for gatherings, meetings and dinners.

RHYTHMISIERUNG DES KORRIDORS

Auch der Korridor, dem im Laufe der Zeit fast alle Jugendstilstuckaturen, die Marmorverkleidungen an den Wänden und viele in Nussbaum gefertigte Originaltüren abhandengekommen waren, brauchte eine innenarchitektonische Klärung. Die verloren gegangene Rhythmisierung wurde mittels aufgesetzten Stuckbändern am Tonnengewölbe wiederhergestellt, die fehlenden Türöffnungen, Türleibungen und Türattrappen wurden ergänzt und fügen sich strukturell in die Sequenz der Wandabschnitte ein. Wenige Farb- und Materialfunde belegen, dass der Marmorbodenbelag, der heute noch zu sehen ist, aus der Bauzeit stammt. Zudem umfasste ein horizontales Brüstungsband aus rötlich orangem Stuckmarmor die Korridorwände.

Bewegt sich der Hotelgast im Korridor an der neu positionierten Rezeption vorbei, gelangt er in den Damensaal und schließlich ins Zentrum des Hotels mit dem ehemaligen Haupteingang, dem Treppenhaus, den Aufzügen und der zum See hin orientierten Hotelhalle. Von hier aus sind auch nach wie vor der neu gestaltete Hotelgarten mit einem Aussenrestaurant und die vorgelagerte Seepromenade erreichbar.

CORRIDOR RHYTHM

The corridor also needed inter-architectural clarification, having lost almost all of its art-nouveau stucco, marble cladding and many of the original walnut doors. Thus the rhythm created by the bands of stucco at the barrel vaults was restored, while missing door apertures, doors jambs and false doors were added, structurally integrating them into the sequence of wall sections. A few original colour and material samples showed that the marble flooring that is still visible today is from the original construction period. A horizontal balustrade band consisting of reddish-orange scagliola ran along the corridor walls.

As guests walk down the corridor, past the newly positioned reception, they reach the ladies' salon and finally the centre of the hotel with its former main entrance, stairs, elevators and the hotel hall orientated towards the lake. The newly designed hotel garden, with its outdoor restaurant and the lakeside promenade, remains accessible from there.

SCHAFFEN EINER NEUEN MITTE DURCH POSITIONIERUNG DER BAR

Die vielen Türen respektive Öffnungen in der Halle – die Mündung des Korridors, der Eingang zur Bar und ins Restaurant, der Ausgang in den Hotelgarten – sowie die raumgreifenden Verkehrswege machten die optimale Möblierung schwierig.

In der Raummitte mit den im Quadrat angeordneten Säulen wurde diese Situation besonders sichtbar. So entstand die Idee, die Hotelbar im Zentrum des Gevierts zu platzieren Die als Oval geformte, grosszügige Bar für hotelinterne und -externe Gäste ist nun das Herz des Hauses. Diese Neupositionierung hatte zur Folge, dass der ehemalige Standort der Bar, ursprünglich der Lesesaal, frei wurde für eine Umnutzung. Der Wunsch der Bauherrschaft war es, ausserdem ein kleines japanisches Restaurant zu betreiben. Als grosses, in den Raum gestelltes «Möbel» konzipiert, wird von hier aus zusätzlich in der Halle bedient. Ein Speiselift verbindet das neue Restaurant mit dem Untergeschoss, wo es eine kleine Fertigungsküche gibt.

VERKLEIDUNG DER LIFTFRONTEN IM ERDGESCHOSS

Auf den historischen Aufnahmen des Korridors von 1906 ist die Holzverkleidung der ehemaligen Conciergekabine zu erahnen. Diese nahm direkten Bezug auf die grossen, in Nussholz gerahmten Verglasungen zur Halle. Aufwendige Holzschnitzereien und Ornamentik im Stil der Belle Époque zierten die über Eck verlaufende Verkleidung. Auch heute nimmt die Gestaltung der Holzfronten Bezug auf die historische Ausgestaltung der Conciergeloge und wird bewusst nicht als Teil der Wand, sondern als Holzeinsatz behandelt, was dem Ort etwas Besonderes verleiht. Die Schnittstelle zur Vertikalerschliessung wird durch eine andere Materialisierung betont. Auch der umlaufende grüne Sockel ist bewusst unterbrochen. Das Ziel, der Haupttreppe ein wertiges, einladendes Gegenüber zu geben, wie das auch schon im Urzustand des Hotels der Fall war, stand im Vordergrund.

THE BAR'S POSITION CREATES A NEW CENTRE

The many doors and apertures in the hall – where the corridor, bar entrance, restaurant entrance and exit to the garden all converge – as well as the extensive walkways, make it difficult to provide ideal furnishing.

This situation is especially conspicuous at the space's centre, where the columns are arranged in a square. It inspired the idea of placing the hotel bar within that quadrangle. Designed as an oval, the spacious bar for hotel guests and members of the public now forms the heart of the building. The repositioning measure freed up the bar's former location in the reading room, which could be reassigned. The client wanted to open a small Japanese eatery in addition to the main restaurant. Conceived as a large piece of "furniture" inserted into the space, the new restaurant also serves customers in the hall. A dumb waiter connects the new restaurant to the basement, where the food is prepared in a small kitchen.

NEW ELEVATOR CLADDING ON THE GROUND FLOOR

Using historical photographs from 1906, it was possible to get a sense of the wooden cladding for the former concierge cabin. They directly referred to the large-scale, walnut-framed glazing in the hall. Elaborate carvings and ornamentation in the Belle Époque style adorned the cladding, which continued round the corner. Today, the design with wooden fronts refers to the historical design of the concierge's office, as it is consciously treated as a wooden inlay rather than part of the wall, representing a special feature for the location. The transition to the vertical access is indicated by the different materialisation. The surrounding green base is also interrupted for that reason. The aim of creating a significant, inviting counterpart to the main stairs was a priority, since it had been the case in the original hotel.

Ansicht Kapo (japanisches Restaurant), Iwan Bühler Architekten, 2021
Front view of the Kapo (Japanese eatery), Iwan Bühler Architekten, 2021

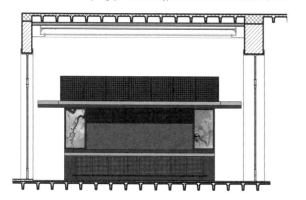

DIE KUNST IM HOTEL PALACE

Hervorragende Malereien mit Landschaftsmotiven waren schon in der Bauzeit ein fester Bestandteil der hoteleigenen Kunstsammlung. Um die Jahrhundertwende, als sich Luzern zu einer boomenden Touristenstadt etabliert hatte, kamen auch die Bewegung an der frischen Luft, Spaziergänge und Wanderungen in der Schweizer Bergwelt in Mode. Neben den Touristenattraktionen, die die Stadt an sich zu bieten hat, wurde die Schönheit der Natur neu entdeckt und als Ausflugsziel angepriesen.

Die grossformatigen Landschaftsbilder waren für die internationalen Gäste Anreize, die Ausflugsziele in der Umgebung zu entdecken und schätzen zu lernen. Bilder bedeutender Künstler wie etwa Johann Gottfried Steffan, Alexandre Calame, Andreas Achenbach, aber auch Varlin (Willy Guggenheim) waren Teil der Sammlung. Bis heute ist ein Grossteil der historischen Kunstsammlung erhalten und kann in den öffentlichen Räumen betrachtet werden.

Auch die die aktuelle, durch zeitgenössische Kunst erweiterte Sammlung thematisiert die Bewahrung der Schweizer Landschaft, ist sie doch nach wie vor ein Aushängeschild für Besucherinnen und Besucher aus aller Welt.

«Die Kunstwerke vergrössern und erforschen spezifische Details der Landschaft – die Felsen, das Licht, das Laub – und bringen ein Gefühl der Wertschätzung für die Details, die das Ganze ausmachen, zum Vorschein, und im Zentrum all dessen steht das Konzept der Menschen in der Natur und unser Umgang mit ihr», beschreiben die Kuratoren Visto die zeitgenössischen Kunstwerke, die den historischen Gemälden gegenübergestellt werden.

ART IN THE HOTEL PALACE

Outstanding paintings with landscape motifs have always been a fixed element of the hotel's own art collection. Around the turn of the century, when Lucerne had established itself as a booming tourist city, exercising in the fresh air, walking and hiking in the Swiss Alpine countryside all became fashionable. In addition to the tourist attractions offered by the city itself, the beauty of the countryside was rediscovered and advertised as a place to go.

The large-format landscape paintings were aimed at inspiring international guests to discover and appreciate the nearby tourist locations. Paintings by important artists such as Johann Gottfried Steffan, Alexandre Calame, Andreas Achenbach and Varlin (Willy Guggenheim) became part of the collection. To this day, a large proportion of the historical art collection has been retained and can be viewed in the public rooms.

Today's collection, which has been supplemented with contemporary artworks, addresses the theme of Swiss nature conservation and remains a highlight for visitors from all around the world.

"The artworks expand on and investigate specific details of the landscape – cliffs, the light, leaves – highlighting a sense of respect for details that combine to create a whole. The focus is always the theme of humans in nature and their approach to it," as the curators Visto describe the contemporary artworks positioned opposite the historical paintings.

DIE ZIMMER IM HOTEL PALACE

Zur historischen Ausgestaltung der Gästezimmer gibt es keinerlei Dokumentationen in den Archiven. Durch die ständigen Renovationen und Modernisierungen der letzten Jahrzehnte, in denen das Hotel für Gäste zugänglich war, war sie nicht mehr rekonstruierbar. Zur Bauzeit waren sämtliche see- und ostseitigen Zimmer mit Privatbädern ausgestattet, welche sich gemeinsam mit den Dienerzimmern um sieben Lichthöfe aneinanderreihten und durch diese belichtet und belüftet werden konnten.

Im Laufe der Jahre etablierte sich das Privatbad zum Standard, weshalb die Gebäudestruktur der Obergeschosse angepasst werden musste. Auch die Lichthöfe fielen den Modernisierungen zum Opfer und sind heute nicht mehr sichtbar. Zugleich stiegen die Anforderungen an Heiz- und Lüftungsanlagen, so dass neue Steigzonen erschlossen werden mussten und der Platzbedarf für Haustechnik und Sanitärinstallationen stetig wuchs. Als das Hotel 2016 geschlossen wurde, gab es schliesslich eine Vielzahl von Ausbauvarianten aus verschiedenen Bauetappen, die keinen Bezug zueinander hatten. So gab es unter anderem noch Zimmer aus den 1970er-Jahren mit mintgrünen Wänden und floralen Stoffbezügen, aber auch in den 2000er-Jahren sanierte, mit blauen Teppichen und rustikalen Holzmöbeln. Es war ein Zufall, in welchem Jahrzehnt sich der Gast in den Zimmern wiederfand und ein Gesamtbild über das Hoteldesign machte.

Heute befinden sich im Hotel Palace 136 Zimmer, darunter 48 Suiten und eine Presidential Suite. Sie wurden gesamtheitlich restauriert und neu interpretiert und orientieren sich an den Farb- und Materialfunden aus der Bauzeit im Erdgeschoss. Unter der Federführung der Londoner Innenarchitekten Jestico + Whiles wurden hochwertige Materialien wie Eichenparkett, Stuckaturen, Naturstein, aber auch Samt, Leinen und Lederstoffe für die Zimmerausstattung verwendet. Die Zimmer und Suiten folgen einem übergeordneten Materialkonzept und unterscheiden sich nur noch geringfügig voneinander, sodass die Sprache der Belle Époque auch in den Zimmern, Bädern und Korridoren zum Ausdruck kommt.

THE HOTEL PALACE'S ROOMS

No archive documentation on the guest rooms' original furnishing has survived. Repeated renovation and modernisation measures in recent decades, whenever the hotel was open to guests, made it impossible to recreate the historical room design. At the time of its construction, all rooms facing the lake and the east enjoyed private bathrooms, which were arranged together with the servants' quarters around seven atria that provided natural light and ventilation.

Over the years, en-suite bathrooms became standard, making it necessary to adapt the building structure on the upper levels. The atria also fell victim to modernisation measures and cannot be seen today. At the same time, heating and ventilation demands increased, requiring access to new riser zones and continually increasing the spatial requirements of the building's technical systems, as well as sanitary installations. When the hotel closed in 2016, there were numerous different versions of fittings from various stages of renovation, none of which related to each other. For instance, there were still rooms from the 1970s, with mint-green walls and floral fabric covers, as well as rooms that had been renovated in the 2000s, with blue carpeting and rustic wooden furniture. Chance would determine the type of room allocated to the guests, affecting their overall impression of the hotel design accordingly.

Today, the Hotel Palace has 136 rooms, including 48 suites and a Presidential Suite. They have been holistically restored and reinterpreted, while being guided by the ground-floor colour and material finds from the original construction period. Under the auspices of the London interior architects Jestico + Whiles, high quality materials such as oak parquet, stucco, natural stone, velvet and different types of leather were all used for the accommodation. The rooms and suites have an overall material concept and vary only slightly from each other, ensuring that the language of the Belle Époque is expressed in all the rooms, bathrooms and corridors.

Zimmer, 1950
Room, 1950

Zimmer, 1970
Room, 1970

Zimmer, 1994
Room, 1994

DER SAAL

«Der unverzichtbare Speisesaal wandelt sich im Verlauf seiner Entwicklung vom einfachen Esszimmer zum prunkvollen Saal. Bis gegen Ende des 19. Jahrhunderts ist es üblich, dass die Hotelgäste zu den Mahlzeiten an langen Tischreihen, der sogenannten Table d'hôte, Platz nehmen. Das Essen wird zu einer bestimmten Uhrzeit aufgetragen, das mehrgängige Menu ist für alle Gäste gleich.

So wurde im Hotel Palace zur Bauzeit neben dem Restaurant ein opulenter Speisesaal im Ostflügel des Gebäudes eingerichtet, der sowohl für Bankette, aber auch für grössere Tanzveranstaltungen genutzt werden konnte. Auffällig ist, dass sich der Speisesaal nicht zur Seeseite hin orientierte und durch eine Erweiterung des Restaurants von der Südfassade abgekoppelt war. «Die Einnahme von Mahlzeiten ist in der Belle Époque ein gesellschaftliches Ereignis des Sehen-und-gesehen-Werdens, das kaum Zeit und Musse für das Geniessen der Aussicht übriglässt», schreibt Peter Omachen in seinem Buch über die Luzerner Hotellerie um die Jahrhundertwende und liefert so eine mögliche Begründung für die spezielle Lage des Saals (Omachen, S. 57).

Da das Hotel bis in die 1970er-Jahre lediglich in der Sommersaison geöffnet war, konnte es in der Zwischensaison umgebaut und renoviert werden. Unter der Leitung des damaligen Direktors Jürg Reinshagen wurden unter anderem der Saal sowie die Hauptküche mit Nebenräumen umgebaut. «Der Umbau des Festsaals folgt dem Wunsch, der wachsenden Nachfrage nach Kongress- und Conventionsräumlichkeiten nachzukommen und hiermit das Angebot des Hotels zu vergrössern», schrieb die damalige Lokalpresse. Weiter heisst es: «Durch den Einbau von mobilen Trennwänden können nun zwei Räumlichkeiten zu je 100 und 150 Sitzplätzen geschaffen werden, was eine Kapazität des gesamten Festsaals von maximal 250 Personen ergibt» (Luzerner Tagblatt, 24. April 1973). Zusätzlich wurde der Saal mit aufwendigen technischen Installationen sowie fest installierten Übersetzerkabinen mit Simultan-Übersetzungsanlagen versehen und dadurch um eine Längsachse verschmälert. Die angrenzende Kücheninfrastruktur wurde vergrössert, um den Anforderungen an den neuen Kongresssaal zu genügen.

Auch statisch und in Bezug auf den Brandschutz zu den darüberliegenden Geschossen stellte der Saal plötzlich eine grosse Herausforderung dar. Aufgrund der Vorgaben im Brandschutz wurden in die filigrane Kassettendeckenkonstruktion aus der Bauzeit zusätzliche Stahlträger eingezogen, die die Decke verstärken. Die grosszügige Raumhöhe büsste dadurch deutlich ein und lässt sich bis heute nur noch anhand der historischen Fotografien erahnen. Heute soll der Saal mehrheitlich für Grossveranstaltungen oder Tagungen genutzt werden. Die Übersetzerkabinen

THE HALL

"The indispensable dining hall has developed over the years from a simple dining room to a sumptuous hall. Until the late 19th century, it was customary for hotel guests to be seated in rows at long dining tables, the so-called *tables d'hôte*. Food was served at a specific time, providing several courses that were the same for all guests."

Thus, when the Hotel Palace was built, an opulent dining hall was designed beside the restaurant in the east wing, which could also be used for banquets and large dance events. It is noticeable that the dining hall was not orientated towards the lake and detached from the restaurant on the southern façade. "During the Belle Époque, meals were a social occasion for seeing and being seen, so one hardly had time to enjoy the view," as Peter Omachen explains in his book on Lucerne's hotel business at the turn of the century, thereby providing a reason for the dining hall's specific location (Omachen, p. 57).

Until the 1970s, the hotel was only open during the summer season, so it was possible to convert and renovate it during the off-season periods. Supervised by the then director Jürg Reinshagen, the hall, main kitchen and auxiliary rooms were among those converted. "The conversion of the festive hall was based on the wish to fulfil growing demand for congress and convention facilities, thereby expanding the range of the hotel's services," as the local press stated at the time. It continues: "The introduction of mobile partition walls permitted two spaces, each with 100 to 150 seats, achieving a capacity of 250 people for the entire festive hall," (*Luzerner Tagblatt*, April 24, 1973). The hall was additionally equipped with extensive technical systems as well as permanently installed interpreters' booths and simultaneous translation systems, thereby narrowing the hall along its longitudinal axis. The adjoining kitchen infrastructure was expanded to cater for the requirements of the new congress hall.

Saal, Heinrich Meili-Wapf, 1906
Hall, Heinrich Meili-Wapf, 1906

wurden entfernt, aber die mobile Zweiteilung des Raumes für mehr Flexibilität beibehalten. Da die bauzeitliche Raumgestaltung durch die vielen Eingriffe längst überformt worden war, wurden Material- und Farbgebung neu interpretiert. Zarte Creme- und Violetttöne nehmen Bezug zur ursprünglichen Fassung und lassen den Raum ruhig und zurückhaltend wirken. Der Saal bietet heute die grösstmögliche technische Ausstattung. So können über private Anlässe mit Bankettbestuhlung und Präsentationen mit Beamer und Leinwand bis hin zu Konzerten Veranstaltungen mit bis zu 300 Personen stattfinden. Durch eine mobile Traversenaufhängung ist es sogar möglich, eine zusätzliche Licht-, Ton- und Kamerainstallation aufzuhängen.

The hall suddenly posed a considerable challenge in terms of the load-bearing structure and fire safety for the floors above it. Due to fire-safety regulations, bracing steel girders were inserted into the finely structured coffered ceiling from the original construction period. The generous room height suffered considerably as a result and can now only be imagined on the basis of historical photographs. Today, the hall is mainly used for major events and conferences. The interpreters' booths have been removed, but the mobile partition has been retained to ensure the space's flexibility. Since the hall's original design had long been transformed by the many measures over the years, the choice of materials and colours was reinterpreted. Soft cream and violet tones refer to the original design, while giving the space a calm, reserved atmosphere. Today's hall offers state-of-the-art technical equipment, enabling private events with banquet seating, presentations with projectors and screens, as well as concerts for up to 300 people. The mobile transverse suspension rig even allows additional lighting, sound and camera installations.

DER STUCKMARMOR IM HOTEL PALACE

Im historischen Hotel Palace von 1906 bediente sich der Architekt einer breiten Farbpalette, die für den damaligen Gast eine exklusive Anmutung gehabt haben muss.

Grosse Wandteile waren mit Marmor verkleidet, wobei es sich allerdings nicht um echten Naturstein handelte, sondern um eine Imitation aus Stuckmarmorierung, die zur damaligen Zeit häufig in repräsentativen Bauten zu finden war und eine günstigere Alternative zum echten Naturstein darstellte. Aufgrund der Gestaltungsmöglichkeiten durch die große Auswahl an Farbgebung und Struktur wurde das Material oftmals dem echten Naturstein vorgezogen.

Stuckmarmor wurde aus Gips, Farbpigmenten sowie Leimwasser zusammengesetzt und in aufwendiger Handarbeit mittels Knetens und Schneidens geformt, anschliessend stückweise auf die Wände aufgetragen, verpresst und poliert. Durch eine Veredelung mit Wachs oder Öl bekam er die typische marmorartige Erscheinung. Spezialisierte Stuckateure konnten ihre Kunstfertigkeit unter Beweis stellen und schufen damit Arbeiten, die den aktuellen Wert von echtem Marmor sogar noch übertreffen. Heute ist das Wissen um das Handwerk leider weitestgehend verloren gegangen und so wird die Technik weltweit nur mehr von sehr wenigen Firmen angewandt. Einige dieser Arbeiten sind im Hotel Palace glücklicherweise erhalten geblieben. So konnten unter den vielen Tapetenschichten im Haupttreppenhaus die originalen Stuckmarmorverkleidungen freigelegt und restauriert werden.

Auch in der Halle (Bar) wurden die Säulen und Wandpilaster erneut aufgearbeitet und vervollständigt, an ihren Wänden befinden sich noch Überreste des olivgrünen und rosa-beigen Stuckmarmors. Dieser wurde jedoch nicht freigelegt, sondern durch eine schützende Schicht aus Vlies konserviert, um auch für künftige Generationen erhalten zu bleiben.

SCAGLIOLA IN THE HOTEL PALACE

The architect who designed the 1906 Hotel Palace used a broad range of colours that must have seemed very luxurious to the guests at the time.

Large wall elements were clad in marble, although these were not made of real natural stone and instead consisted of artificial scagliola, which was often used at the time for prestigious buildings and was a more affordable alternative to real natural stone. Due its design possibilities and the wide range of colours and structure, the material was often preferred to real natural stone.

Scagliola was made of plaster, colour pigments and stickwater. Its production involved a laborious manual process of kneading and cutting, before it was applied to the walls in sections, pressed and polished. Refinement with wax or oil gave it a typical marble-like appearance. At the time, stucco specialists were able to demonstrate their skill in creating works that were actually more valuable than real marble. Today, the know-how and craftsmanship has largely been lost, since only a very few firms around the world still use the technique. Fortunately, one of these scagliola works had remained preserved in the Hotel Palace. The original scagliola design was exposed from beneath the main staircase's many layers of wallpaper and could be restored.

The columns and wall pilasters in the hall (bar) were also restored and completed. Their walls still revealed remnants of the original olive-green and rose-beige scagliola. However, instead of exposing them, they were preserved in a protective fleece material to ensure their survival for future generations.

Grafische Darstellung der Original-farben von 1906, Iwan Bühler Architekten 2019
Graphic presentation of the original 1906 colours, Iwan Bühler Architekten, 2019

DIE INNENTÜREN

Die letzte erhaltene Tür aus der Bauzeit befand sich an der Ostwand des Damensaals und diente, gemeinsam mit den Fotografien von 1906, als Grundlage für die Neuinterpretationen der Bogentüren und der grossen Verglasungen in allen öffentlichen Räumen. Der restauratorische Farbuntersuch sowie die Aufnahmen ergaben eine Materialisierung aus Nussbaumholz mit rötlichem Anstrich sowie Stossgriffe und Trittschutz aus Messing. Die Gläser waren teilweise satiniert. Die historischen Türen besassen Steinfaschen aus hellem Carrara Marmor. Für den Sockelstein wählte der Architekt Meili-Wapf einen dunkelgrünen Gotthardserpentin, der auch heute noch in kleinen Mengen im Kanton Uri abgebaut wird, und bildete damit den Übergang zum ebenfalls dunkelgrünen Stuckmarmor-Sockel, welcher sämtliche Säle umfasste.

Die historischen Steinfaschen wurden jeweils mit einem vergoldeten Kapitell auf einer Höhe von circa 3,10 Meter abgeschlossen Die Bögen darüber waren aus Stuck mit kunstvollen Vergoldungen und verspielten Ornamenten. Die Kapitelle bildeten die Schnittstelle zum umlaufenden Horizont, der vor allem in Halle, Lesesaal und Veranda sichtbar war. Dieser spielt mit der Raumwahrnehmung des Gastes: Durch die Anhebung des Horizonts über Kopfhöhe wurde der Raum vertikal gegliedert und die opulente Raumhöhe inszeniert. Das Thema des umlaufenden Horizonts wurde in der Halle (Bar) wirkungsvoll wiederaufgenommen und findet seinen Ausdruck in der nördlichen Verglasung zum Korridor und den Fenstern der Südfassade.

Im Laufe der Bauarbeiten kam es zu einem bedeutenden Fund, als unter der ehemaligen Haupttreppe im Untergeschoss die bauzeitlichen Marmorfaschen, die einst die grossen Bogentüren zierten, gefunden wurden; ein glücklicher Zufall, dass ihr Wert bei damaligen Umbauten bereits erkannt wurde und sie eingelagert und nicht rücksichtslos entsorgt worden waren. Unter Beizug des Steinrestaurators Vitus Wey konnte ein Teil der Faschen wieder restauriert und im Damensaal eingebaut werden. Die weiteren Türeinfassungen im Erdgeschoss wurden als Holzfaschen neu interpretiert. Dabei wurde sehr viel Wert auf die formale Detaillierung der Materialfügungen gelegt. So wurde das Fugenbild der bauzeitlichen Türeinfassungen, also Steinfasche zu Holzleibung zu Schlussstein aus Gotthardserpentin weitgehend beibehalten. Dies ermöglichte es auch, den Farb- und Materialwechsel zwischen den Räumen und Korridoren elegant aufzunehmen. Die Proportionen der Türen mussten sich teilweise den neuen Raumhöhen im Korridor anpassen. Während die historischen Türen eine lichte Bogenhöhe von ca. 4,10 Meter aufwiesen, mussten die korridorseitigen Türen auf eine Bogenhöhe von 3,70 Meter reduziert werden.

INTERIOR DOORS

The last remaining original door was situated on the eastern wall of the ladies' salon and, together with photographs from 1906, formed the basis of arched doors and the large glazed areas in all public spaces. The restorer's colour analysis and the photos found that walnut wood had been used, with brass push handles and skirting. Some of the glazing was satin-finished. The historical doors included stone surrounds made of light-coloured Carrara marble. The architect Meili-Wapf chose a dark green Gotthard Serpentine for the base stone, which is still quarried in small amounts in the Canton of Uri. It forms the transition to the scagliola base in all the salons and is also dark green.

The historical stone surrounds included gold-leafed capitals at a height of around 3.10 metres. The arches above them consisted of stucco with artistic gold-leaf decoration and playful ornamentation. The capitals mediate with the surrounding horizon that was above all visible in the hall, reading room and veranda. It plays on the guests' spatial perception, since it structured the room vertically, while its opulent height was accentuated by placing the horizon above head height. The theme of the surrounding horizon in the hall (bar) was used to good effect and is expressed in the northern glazing towards the corridor and the south-façade windows.

A significant discovery was made during building work, as the original marble surrounds were discovered beneath the main stairs in the basement. They had once decorated the large arched doors; it was fortunate that their value was recognised during conversion work at the time, and that the surrounds were put into storage rather than being carelessly discarded. With support from the stone restorer Vitus Wey, part of the surrounds were restored and installed in the ladies' salon. The other door surrounds on the ground floor were newly interpreted in wood. Great efforts were made with respect to the formal details of the material joints. In this way, it was possible to retain the joint structure of the original door fittings, consisting of a stone surround, a wooden jamb and the base stone made of Gotthard Serpentine. This also made it possible to elegantly pick up on the alternating colours and materials between the rooms and the corridors. Some door dimensions had to be adapted to the new room heights. While the arches of the historical doors had a clearance height of 4.10 metres, the doors on the corridor side had to be reduced due to an arch clearance height of 3.70 metres.

Wiederverwendete, im Estrich eingelagerte Original Marmorfaschen von 1906, Iwan Bühler Architekten, 2019
Re-used, original marble surrounds from 1906, stored in the screed, Iwan Bühler Architekten, 2019

STOSSGRIFFE

Die historischen Stossgriffe waren zu zwei Kreis-bögen geformte Rundrohre. Zudem verliefen zwei horizontale Griffstangen zu den Aussenkanten der Türen. Diese nahmen die umlaufende Horizontale des Korridors auf Hüfthöhe des Gastes auf. Da auf die Horizontale in der Neuinterpretation des Korridors nicht mehr Bezug genommen werden konnte, hat man sich dafür entschieden, den Stossgriff neu zu interpretieren. Zudem gab es neue Anforderungen an die Türen, die ursprünglich einfache Doppelpendeltüren gewesen waren, hinsichtlich Zugangskontrollen, Brandschutz beziehungsweise Fluchtwegen sowie Schallschutz, welche der Ausgestaltung nach historischem Vorbild entgegenstanden.

PUSH HANDLES

The historical push handles consisted of circular tubes shaped into two arcs. Two horizontal hand rails also ran towards the doors' outer edges. They assumed the surrounding horizontal corridor element at the guests' hip height. Since the corridor's new interpretation could no longer refer to the horizontal element, it was decided to reinterpret the push handles. The doors had to fulfil new requirements: the originals had been simple double swing-doors, but the new design could not be based on its predecessors due to aspects of access control, fire safety and noise insulation.

Türe zur Rezeption, 2022
Door to the Reception area, 2022

Historischer Stossgriff, 1906
Historical push handle, 1906

Neuinterpretation Stossgriff, 2022
Reinterpreted push handle, 2022

Originaltüre Damensaal, 1906
Original door, ladies' salon, 1906

DAS LICHTKONZEPT

André Bachmann und Andrea Peyer

LIGHTING CONCEPT

André Bachmann and Andrea Peyer

André Bachmann
* 1971, Lichtplanung LICHTTEAM AG
Andrea Peyer
*1968, Lichtplanung LICHTTEAM AG

André Bachmann
Born in 1971, lighting planning,
LICHTTEAM AG
Andrea Peyer
Born in 1968, lighting planning,
LICHTTEAM AG

Der Fortschrittsglaube «Wissenschaft durch Technik» war typisch in der Zeit der Belle Époque und bezeichnend für den Komfort des Hotel Palace während der Bauzeit. In Zeiten des wirtschaftlichen Aufschwungs wollte man sich das Leben behaglich einrichten und den Wohlstand zur Schau stellen.

Der elektrische Strom löste die zweite industrielle Revolution aus. In der Schweiz hielt diese neue Technologie über den Tourismus sehr früh Einzug. An Weihnachten 1878 brannte im Speisesaal des Kulm Hotel in St. Moritz erstmals elektrisches Licht. Der neue Luxus war in der Folge unverzichtbar für alle Grand Hotels. Die Oberschicht konnte sich mit elektrischem Licht sozial abgrenzen, kostete die Kilowattstunde Elektrizität damals doch rund den vierfachen Stundenlohn eines gelernten Arbeiters. Ab 1885 war die aufstrebende Tourismusdestination Luzern einer der ersten Orte mit elektrischem Licht in den Hotels, zur Beleuchtung von Sehenswürdigkeiten und Strassen. Ab 1899 verkehrte mit den Linien Halde-Obergrund und Maihof-Kreuzstutz die erste elektrisch betriebene Trambahn.

Das Hotel Palace bot bei der Eröffnung extraganten Luxus. Dazu zählte auch die elektrische Beleuchtung im ganzen Haus. Die ersten Glühlampen waren zwar ein technisches Wunderwerk, nach heutigen Massstäben aber sehr ineffizient. Sie gaben ein vergleichsweise schwa-

Faith in the progress of "science through technology" was typical of the Belle Époque period and characterised the comfort-features in the Hotel Palace during its construction period. In times of economic boom, the aim was to make life comfortable and flaunt one's prosperity.

Electricity sparked off the second industrial revolution. In Switzerland, the new technology had a very early effect on tourism. During the Christmas season in 1878, the dining hall in Kulm Hotel, St. Moritz was illuminated by electric light for the first time. The new luxury subsequently became essential for all grand hotels. Electric light set the upper class apart, since at the time, a kilowatt hour of electricity cost a skilled labourer around four hours' wages. From 1885, the booming tourist destination of Lucerne was one of the first locations with electric light in its hotels, as well as using it to illuminate sight-seeing attractions and streets. From 1899, the first electrically powered trams were operated on the city's Halde-Obergrund and Maihof-Kreuzstutz lines.

When it opened, Hotel Palace offered extravagant luxury. That included electric light in the entire building. The first lightbulbs were a technical miracle, but very inefficient by today's standards. They were relatively dim, created a large amount of heat and were extremely sensitive to fluctuating currents and vibrations. Thus they needed frequent replacement. As a result, lights and luminaires had to be constructed in a user-friendly way, with easily accessible fittings.

**Achtarmiger Kristallleuchter Restaurant,
wiederverwendet**
Eight-armed crystal luminaire for the
restaurant, re-used

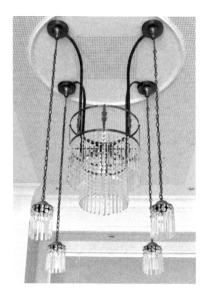

**Vierarmiger Kristallleuchter Restaurant,
wiederverwendet**
Four-armed crystal luminaire for the
restaurant, re-used

ches Licht, erzeugten viel Wärme und waren gegen Spannungsschwankungen und Erschütterungen äusserst empfindlich, ein häufiger Wechsel der Glühmittel war erforderlich. Entsprechend mussten die Leuchten und Leuchter bedienungsfreundlich konstruiert und die Lampenfassungen leicht zugänglich sein.

Während in der Halle und in den Sälen eher schlichte Ringleuchter mit grosszügigen Durchmessern eingesetzt wurden, waren es im Damensaal elektrifizierte Kronleuchter und in den Speisesälen Lichtskulpturen mit geschwungenen Linien und floralen Elementen. Die Korridore wurden mit laternenartigen Opalglas-Leuchten und Plafonieren beleuchtet. Für die Zeit typisch waren der «moderne» Stil, die Funktionalität und die Verwendung der für die aufkommende Massenproduktion typischen Materialen wie Eisen, Industriekeramik und halbmaschinell gefertigte Hohlgläser.

Von der historischen Beleuchtung sind heute einzig die Leuchter im Damensaal erhalten. Bei den wiederverwendeten Lichtskulpturen im Restaurant handelt es sich um bereits während einer früheren Renovation gefertigte Nachbauten der Originale.

Das aktuelle Lichtkonzept der öffentlichen Räume wurde durch die Lichtplaner der LICHTTEAM AG in enger Zusammenarbeit mit den Architekten und der Denkmalpflege entwickelt. Historische Elemente wurden aufwendig restauriert und kommen an ihrem ursprünglichen Standort wieder zum Einsatz.

Zur Erreichung der heutigen Normvorgaben und Ansprüche an eine homogene und blend-

While simple ring luminaires with generous diameters were installed in the hall and larger rooms, the ladies' salon used electric chandeliers and the dining rooms contained light sculptures with sweeping lines and floral elements. The corridors were equipped with lantern-like opal glass lights and *plafoniers*. The "modern" style was typical of the time, combining function with materials associated with emerging mass production, such as iron, industrial ceramics and semi-automatically manufactured hollow glassware.

The lamps in the ladies' salon are the only surviving original lighting. The re-used lighting sculptures in the restaurant are copies of the originals produced during previous refurbishing work.

The current lighting concept for the public rooms was developed by the lighting planners of the LICHTTEAM AG in close collaboration with the architects and the monument preservation authority. Historical elements were laboriously restored and returned to their original location.

To achieve today's standards and fulfil the demand for even, non-dazzling light, the basic lighting was supplemented with ceiling lights and indirect lighting in the coves. The lamps in the hall and corridor had been removed during earlier renovation work. Replicas were not an option, so the new lighting concept is a modern interpretation of the original fittings, as documented in historical photographs. The materialisation in brass and opal diffusers was repeated in homage to the original. Alabaster and blown opal glass were used as decorative elements.

The luminaires over the large bar at the centre of the hall were specially produced by the craftsman and lighting constructor David Szarka. The simple, triple-layer luminaire ensures atmospheric light. Its

**Kristallleuchter Damensaal,
wiederverwendet und ergänzt**
Crystal luminaire for the ladies' salon,
re-used and augmented

**Kristallleuchter Vestibule,
wiederverwendet**
Crystal luminaire for the vestibule,
re-used

freie Beleuchtung wurde die Grundbeleuchtung mit Deckeneinbauleuchten und Indirektbeleuchtung in den Vouten ergänzt. Die Leuchter in der Halle und im Korridor des Erdgeschosses fielen früheren Renovationen zum Opfer. Nachbauten waren keine Option. Das neue Lichtkonzept ist eine moderne Interpretation der ursprünglichen Ausstattung, wie sie in historischen Aufnahmen dokumentiert ist. Die Materialisierung in Messing und opalen Diffusoren wurde als Reminiszenz übernommen. Als dekorative Elemente kommen Alabaster und mundgeblasene Opalgläser zum Einsatz.

Der Leuchter über der grossen Bar im Zentrum der Halle ist eine Mass-Anfertigung, ausgeführt durch den Kunsthandwerker und Leuchtenbauer David Szarka. Der schlichte dreistufige Ringleuchter ermöglicht eine stimmungsvolle Barbeleuchtung. Mit seiner Dimension und der als dekoratives Oblicht gefertigten Plafoniere stärkt er das Raumzentrum und unterstützt durch seine filigrane Bauweise die Lesbarkeit der ursprünglichen lichtdurchfluteten Empfangshalle mit dem einzigartigen Blick hinaus auf den See und die Berge.

Die Beleuchtung in der neuen Rezeption, dem Bankett- und Ballsaal und den seeseitigen Wintergärten ist mit Leuchten aktueller Designer und Hersteller ausgeführt, die alle mit hochwertiger LED-Technologie ausgerüstet sind. Die Lichtfarben und die Helligkeit lassen sich der Nutzung und den gewünschten Stimmungen entsprechend anpassen.

dimensions and a *plafonier* designed as a decorative skylight strengthen the spatial centre, while its delicate construction supports the legibility of the original light-flooded reception hall, with its unique view of the lake and mountains.

The lighting in the new reception area, as well as for the banquet hall and the lakeside conservatory, is equipped with lights by contemporary designers and manufacturers, all using high-quality LED technology. The tone and brightness of the light can be adjusted to suit the respective use and desired atmosphere.

Kronleuchter über der Bar, David Szarka, 2022
Entwurf von Iwan Bühler Architekten und LICHTTEAM AG, 2022
Luminaires over the bar, David Szarka, 2022
Design by Iwan Bühler Architekten and LICHTTEAM AG, 2022

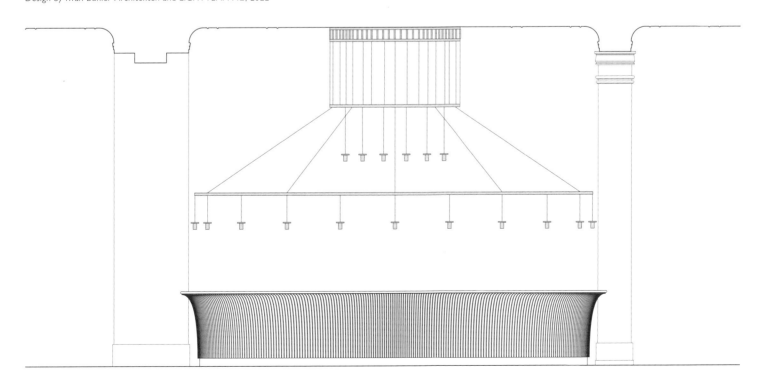

DIE STOFFE IM DAMENSAAL

Birgit Roller

THE FABRICS IN THE LADIES' SALON

Birgit Roller

Bereits bei Eröffnung des Hotels waren die Wände des Damensaals von gewobenen roten Jacquardstoffen mit opulenter Ornamentik geziert. Die Farbkombinationen mit rotem Stoff und den dunkelgrün marmorierten Sockelelementen, aber auch edlen Goldverzierungen und Stuckaturen waren typisch für den damals populären Jugendstil oder auch Art Nouveau und galten in der gehobenen Hotellerie als exklusive Ausdrucksform. In Zusammenarbeit mit dem Textildesigner Bernhard Duss wurden die neuen Stoffbespannungen speziell für den Damensaal neu konzipiert und nach historischem Vorbild interpretiert.

Die Lilie als Symbol für Schönheit und Weiblichkeit, welche um die Jahrhundertwende auch im Hotel als Ornament zum Einsatz kam, galt als passendes Gestaltungselement für den ehemaligen Damensaal. Der Einsatz von glänzenden Goldfäden auf einem matten Wollstoff spielt bewusst mit der Kontrastwirkung beider Materialien. Die Blüten sind in drei Goldtönen dreidimensional übereinandergestickt und lassen die Liliensymbolik effektvoll in den Vordergrund treten. Die Musterwiederholung der aufsteigenden Blüten stellte eine enorme Herausforderung für die 15 Meter lange Strickmaschine der St. Galler Firma Bischoff dar. Sie verarbeitete ca. 500 000 Meter Goldfaden, was einer Strecke von Luzern nach Paris entspricht. Edle cremefarbene seidig glänzende Stoffe der historischen Bogentüren sowie ein neuer handgetufteter dunkelgrüner Teppich ergänzen den exklusiven Ausdruck des Saals und nehmen direkten Bezug auf die historische Farbgebung.

When the hotel was opened, the walls of the ladies' salon were already covered in woven red Jacquard materials with opulent ornamentation. The colour combination with red fabric and the dark green marble-patterned base elements, as well as the refined gold decoration and stucco, were all typical of the Empire style that was popular at the time, as well as *arts décoratifs*, and were regarded as an expression of exclusivity in the luxury hotel sector. The new fabric cover by the textile designer Bernhard Duss was specially conceived for the ladies' salon, reinterpreting historical examples.

The lily, a symbol of beauty, femininity and vanity, which was also used as ornamentation in the hotel around the turn of the century, was regarded as a suitable leitmotif for the former ladies' salon. The shiny gold threads on the matte woollen material consciously play on the contrasting effects of both materials. The petals are embroidered over each other in three dimensions and in three different gold tones, thereby highlighting the lily symbolism. The repetition of the pattern for the ascending flowers posed an enormous challenge to the 15-metre-long embroidery machine owned by the St. Gallen-based company Bischoff. It used around 500,000 metres of gold thread, roughly the distance between Lucerne and Paris. Elegant cream-coloured brocade materials to obscure the historical arch doors and a new hand-tufted, dark-green carpet complement the exclusive expression of the salon, referring directly to the historical colour scheme.

Birgit Roller.
*1959, Innenarchitektin, Inhaberin Casa Tessuti

Birgit Roller.
Born in 1959, interior architect, owner of the Casa Tessuti

Damensaal, Heinrich Meili-Wapf, 1906
Ladies' salon, Heinrich Meili-Wapf, 1906

Damensaal, Blickrichtung Süden, 2016
Ladies' salon, looking south, 2016

Damensaal, Detailaufnahme Goldfaden, 2021
Ladies' salon, detail, gold thread, 2021

Damensaal, Produktion Goldstickerei, 2021
Ladies' salon, gold embroidery production, 2021

EIN HISTORISIERENDER SCHMUCKGARTEN DES FRÜHEN 20. JAHRHUNDERTS

Sven Reithel

Während der Belle Époque wurden die grossen, herrschaftlichen Hotels zu Palästen des Bürgertums. Ein niedriger, geschmiedeter Hag begrenzte die Gartenterrasse des Hotel Palace und «schützte» die gut betuchten Hotelgäste vor dem einfachen Volk – ohne den Blick über den See zu verstellen.

Die Terrasse ist dem Hotel südseitig vorgelagert. Auf historischen und idealisierten Postkarten trumpft dieser schmale Streifen mit einer Fülle an bunten Blumenarrangements und schmückenden mediterranen Pflanzen auf und wird trotz seiner geringen Grösse dem herrschaftlichen und prächtigen Charakter des Hotelbaus gerecht. Die exakte und formale Gliederung der Fläche durch vier rechteckige Parterres entspricht der Gestaltungssprache des Neobarocks und steht damit in einem direkten Bezug zum Baustil des Hotels.

In der Garten- und Landschaftsarchitektur des ausgehenden 19. und beginnenden 20. Jahrhunderts wurden zunehmend bisherige Gestaltungsprinzipien hinterfragt. Formale und strenge Elemente früherer Epochen wurden wieder modern und fanden so Eingang in die Gartenplanung des Palace-Hotels. Gleichwohl zeugen die historischen Abbildungen von einem wertvollen und repräsentativen Aussenraum: Die vier Parterres waren allseitig von chaussierten Wegen umgeben und als üppige «Teppichbeete» angelegt. Wechselnde Blumenarrangements mit kräftigen Farben und grossen Kontrasten zeichneten zierende Muster in die Schmuckpflanzungen. Die Bepflanzung erfolgte saisonal und überraschte zu jeder Jahreszeit mit neuer Farbenpracht. Diese attraktiven Blumenrabatten ähnelten jenen ornamentalen Teppichbeeten, die auch um die Jahrtausendwende in Mode waren. Geschnittene, immergrüne Pflanzbänder rahmten die Beetstrukturen und den Gartenraum, eine niedrige Mauer mit dekorativen Zaunelementen schloss ihn zur Seepromenade hin ab.

A HISTORICISING ORNAMENTAL GARDEN FROM THE EARLY 20TH CENTURY

Sven Reithel

During the Belle Époque, large, stately hotels became bourgeois palaces. A low, forged balustrade outlined the Hotel Palace's garden terrace, "protecting" the well-to-do hotel guests from the simple folk without obstructing the view over the lake.

The terrace is in front of the hotel's south side. On historical and idealised postcards, this narrow strip is presented with a wealth of colourful flower arrangements and decorative Mediterranean plants, thereby making a suitable contribution to the magnificently prestigious character of the hotel building, despite its small size. The exact and formal division of the area into four rectangular parterres corresponds to the design language of the Neo-Baroque. It is thus directly related to the architectural style of the hotel.

In landscape architecture around the turn of the 19th and 20th centuries, there was an increasing break with the traditions of the two previous centuries; formal, austere elements became modern again and thus found their way into the garden of the Palace Hotel. At the same time, historical images of the hotel reveal the valuable, prestigious exterior space: the parterre areas were surrounded on all sides by macadamised walkways and designed as lush so-called carpet beds. Changing annual plant arrangements with bold colours and strong contrasts drew ornamental patterns in the decorative plantings, which were seasonal and surprised with a new blaze of colour every year. These attractive flower borders resembled the ornamental carpet beds that were also in fashion at the turn of the century. Cut, evergreen plant bands framed the beds and the garden room, while a low wall with decorative fence elements closed it off from the lake promenade.

Sven Reithel.
*1987, Landschaftsarchitekt und Fachbereichsleiter Gartendenkmalpflege, SKK Landschaftsarchitekten Wettingen

Sven Reithel.
Born in 1987, landscape architect and Head of Department in conservation of historical gardens, SKK Landschaftsarchitekten Wettingen

Garten, 1906, kolorierte Postkarten
Garden, 1906, coloured postcards

Lucerne. Palace Hôtel.

Lucerne. Palace Hôtel.

NEUE ANSPRÜCHE UND HEUTIGE REPRÄSENTATIVE GESTALTUNG

Die Neugestaltung der Gartenterrasse nimmt Bezug auf auf den historischen Schmuckgarten, wird aber auch den betrieblichen Erfordernissen gerecht. Die ursprünglichen Parterres sind nun als zwei Restaurations- und zwei Gartenparterres erlebbar. Der hochwertige Pflasterbelag aus heimischem Quarzsandstein aus dem Steinbruch Guber hoch über dem Alpnachersee zeichnet durch einen Formatwechsel auf ein kleinteiligeres Muster die früheren Parterres und heutigen Restaurantterrassen nach. Eine besondere Auszeichnung erfährt der Zugangsbereich: Immergrüne Magnolien in grossen Holztrögen und ein von einer üppigen Pflanzung umgebener Brunnen laden Passantinnen und Passanten ein, das Hotel und seinen Garten zu besuchen.

Die äusseren Parterres wurden in Reminiszenz an die ursprüngliche Gestaltung mit jeweils einer grosszügigen Blumenrabatte, die jede Saison neu bepflanzt wird, ausstaffiert, die beiden mehrstämmigen Judasbäume im Zentrum der Gärten überzeugen mit ihrer schönen Blüte und ansprechenden Herbstfärbung. Bepflanzung und Artenwahl des Gartens greifen im Hotel gefundene Motive wie die Lilie oder Palmen auf.

Die bunten Wechselflorrabatten werden von einer zurückhaltenden Pflanzung begleitet. Es überwiegen gelbe Blütenfarben und sattes Grün. Die harmonisch aufeinander abgestimmten gelben Blütentöne spannen einen visuellen Bogen zur Farbe des Hauses und sind komplementär zum Blau des Vierwaldstättersees. Die neu gestaltete Hotelterrasse ist zum einen floral geschmückter Ort der Aussengastronomie an der Seepromenade, zum anderen wird der Gast an die Pracht des früheren Hotelgartens erinnert und kann so auf den Spuren der Belle Époque wandeln.

NEW DEMANDS AND CONTEMPORARY PRESTIGIOUS DESIGN

The redesign of the garden terraces refers to the historical ornamental gardens, but also meets operational requirements. The original terraces or parterres can now be experienced as two restoration parterres and two garden parterres. The high-quality paving, made of local quartz stone from the Guber quarry high above Lake Alpnach, traces the former parterres and current restaurant terraces by changing the format to a small-scale pattern. A unique feature is the entrance area: evergreen magnolias in large wooden troughs and a fountain surrounded by lush planting invite passers-by to visit the hotel and its garden.

The outer parterres have been decorated in reminiscence to the original design, each with a generous flower border that is replanted every season. The two multi-stemmed Judas trees in the centre of the gardens captivate with their beautiful blossoms and appealing autumn colours. The garden's planting and species selection reflects motifs in the hotel, such as the lily or palms.

The colourful annual flowerbeds are accompanied by calmer and simpler planting. Yellow flower colours and lush green predominate. The harmoniously coordinated flowers in different shades of yellow form a visual connection to the house's façade colour and are complementary to the blue of Lake Lucerne.On the one hand, the newly designed hotel terrace is a florally decorated place for outdoor dining on the lakeside promenade, while on the other hand, a reminder for all guests of the the former hotel garden's splendour, allowing anyone to walk in the footsteps of the Belle Époque.

Aussenterrasse mit öffentlicher Uferpromenade, Iwan Bühler Architekten und SKK Landschaftsarchitekten, 2021
Exterior terrace with public lakeside promenade, Iwan Bühler Architekten and SKK Lanschaftsarchitekten, 2021

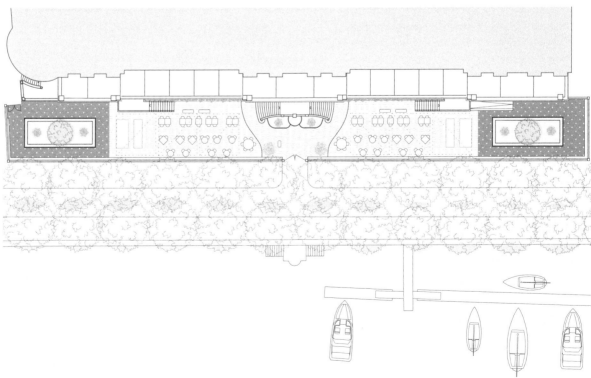

BESTAND UND NEUESTE TECH-NOLOGIEN VERSCHMELZEN

Silvan Birrer

In den letzten Jahren haben sich nicht nur die Raumnutzungen des Gebäudes, sondern auch die Anforderungen und Richtlinien der Normen stark verändert. Als oberstes Ziel galt es, die neue HLKKS-Technik (Heizung-Lüftung-Klima-Kälte-Sanitär) so ins Gebäude zu integrieren, dass man allen Bedürfnissen gerecht wird und der Charme des altehrwürdigen Gebäudes trotzdem erhalten bleibt. In einem integralen Planungsprozess mit den Architekten, den Planungspartnern, der Denkmalpflege und den Anforderungen der Behörden wurde intensiv nach optimalen Lösungen gesucht.

Einen besonders ausführlichen Austausch erforderte der Damensaal, der neubenannte Salon Alpin. Die bestehenden Decken und Wände durften möglichst nicht angerührt werden. Schmale Zuluftgitter wurden präzis über die restaurierten Wandbespannungen gesetzt. Die Abluft wird über die Schattenfugen der Wandbespannungen abgeführt. All diese Aspekte haben eine komplette Überarbeitung der HLKKS-Konzepte in diesem Bereich sowie in den Geschossen darüber und darunter nach sich gezogen.

Im Restaurant wurden die Auslässe für die Zuluft in der Decke im Bereich der Stuckelemente gesetzt, sodass das Deckenbild nicht gestört wird. Die Abluftauslässe wiederum wurden im horizontalen Deckenversatz nur wo notwendig und möglichst reduziert platziert. Dem Wunsch der Bauherrschaft, ein kleines japanisches Restaurant zu betreiben, wurde nachgekommen. Dieses ist neben der Bar westseitig im ehemaligen Lesezimmer zu finden. Ein grosses in den Raum gestelltes «Möbel» wird auch als Satellitenküche genutzt. Weil der bestehende Raum nicht tangiert werden durfte, war die Integration der Lüftung ins Möbel sehr komplex.

In vielen Einzelschritten wurden die HLKKS-Entwürfe für die einzelnen Nutzungen optimiert und in enger Zusammenarbeit mit dem Planungsteam und den Unternehmern vor Ort weiterentwickelt, bis die bestmögliche Lösung vorlag.

Dies sind nur wenige Beispiele, die aufzeigen sollen, wie anspruchsvoll diese Aufgabe war. Ausgerüstet mit der neuesten Technologie erstrahlt das Hotel aus der Belle Époque nun in neuem Glanz und erfüllt alle an das Gebäude gestellten Anforderungen.

MERGING NEW TECHNOLOGY WITH OLD STRUCTURES

Silvan Birrer

In recent years, not only the building's uses, but also its standard regulations and guidelines have changed considerably. The primary aim was to integrate the HVAC (heating, ventilation, air-conditioning) and sanitary systems into the building to fulfil current demands, while still preserving the charm of the venerable building. Ideal solutions were intensively sought in an integral planning process involving the architects, planning partners, monument preservation authority and the requirements of other official bodies.

The ladies' salon, now known as the Salon Alpin, required especially extensive interaction. The existing ceilings and walls had to remain untouched as far as possible. Narrow air-supply grates were precisely placed above the restored wall covering, while extracted air was passed through its shadow gaps. All these aspects required a complete amendment of the HVAC concepts in this building section, as well as on the floors above and below.

In the restaurant, the vents for the air supply in the ceiling were placed near the stucco elements, to avoid undermining the appearance of the ceiling. The vents for the extracted air were positioned in the horizontal ceiling-offset. It was possible to fulfil the client's wish to establish a small Japanese restaurant in the salon, which is now situated beside the bar, on its western side in the former reading room. A large piece of "furniture" was inserted into the space and can also be used as a satellite kitchen. Since the existing salon could not be altered, the ventilation had to be integrated into the furniture in a highly complex process.

In many individual steps, the HVAC and sanitary designs for the separate uses were optimised and developed further in close collaboration with the planning team and the companies working on-site, until the best possible solution was reached.

These are only a few examples that demonstrate the challenging nature of the task. Equipped with state-of-the-art technology, the Belle Époque hotel now shines in new splendour, fulfilling all of its requirements.

Silvan Birrer (Projektleiter HLKKS). *1982, Geschäftsleitung & Senior Partner, W&P Engineering AG

Silvan Birrer (Project Manager, HVACS). Born in 1982, Managing Director & Senior Partner, W&P Engineering AG

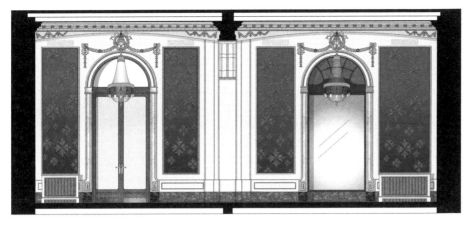

Damensaal, Ansicht West, Iwan Bühler Architekten, 2021
Ladies' salon, view to the west, Iwan Bühler Architekten, 2021

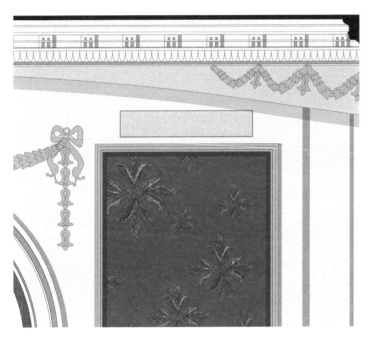

Detailansicht Zu- und Abluft, Iwan Bühler Architekten, 2021
Detail, air inflow and outflow, Iwan Bühler Architekten, 2021

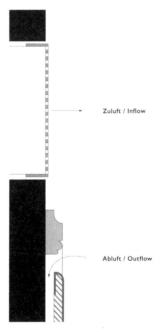

Zuluft / Inflow

Abluft / Outflow

Detailschnitt Zu- und Abluft, Iwan Bühler Architekten, 2021
Detail, sectional view, air inflow and outflow, Iwan Bühler Architekten, 2021

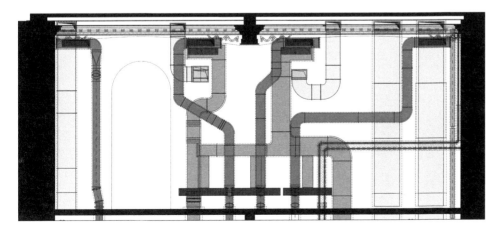

Heizung / Heating

Zuluft / Air inflow

Abluft / Air outflow

Sanitär / Sanitary

Schema Haustechnik, Installationswand zwischen Damensaal und Rezeption, W&P 2021
Scheme of the building technology, installation wall between the ladies' salon and the Reception area, W&P 2021

EIN HAUCH BELLE ÉPOQUE KEHRT ZURÜCK

Cony Grünenfelder

EINE DENKMALPFLEGERISCHE ERNEUERUNG

Mein erstes Gespräch mit dem Bauherrn und dem Architekten fand 2015 im Restaurant «Marlin» im Hotel Palace statt. Entlang der Seepromenade kommend wirkte es auf den ersten Blick von aussen weitgehend unverändert und intakt auf mich. Beim Hotel angelangt, betrat ich das Gebäude durch den heutigen Haupteingang an der Westseite, ging den langen Korridor entlang, bis ich in die grosszügige Eingangshalle gelangte. Es gab keinen Hinweis, wo sich das Restaurant befand, und so lief ich zurück durch sämtliche Erdgeschossräume, die ich entlang der Schaufassade zum See aufgereiht vorfand, bis ich mich schlussendlich wieder am Ausgangspunkt befand. Ein Hotelangestellter führte mich dann ins Restaurant. Dieses Erlebnis war bezeichnend für die Situation, wie sich das Erdgeschoss des Hotels vor dem Umbau präsentierte. Die Raumabfolge war unübersichtlich und die einzelnen Räume verbaut. Die Archivrecherchen des Architekten Iwan Bühler bestätigten später diesen ersten Eindruck: Die öffentlich zugänglichen Erdgeschossräume waren seit der Eröffnung des Hotels 1906 in regelmässigen Abständen mehrfach baulich verändert und umgestaltet worden, dabei wurde meist keine Rücksicht auf die handwerkliche und gestalterische Qualität der bauzeitlichen Ausstattung genommen. Durch die schleichende Purifizierung im Laufe der Zeit verloren die Räume nicht nur ihre historischen Oberflächen, sondern auch ihren Charakter. Aufgrund der bauhistorischen Analyse waren wir uns nach den ersten Gesprächen einig, dass in den öffentlich zugänglichen Räumen im Erdgeschoss die noch vorhandenen historischen Spuren wieder freigelegt und sichtbar gemacht werden sollten, um damit wieder einen Hauch Belle Époque spürbar werden zu lassen.

DAS DENKMALPFLEGERISCHE KONZEPT

Das Hotel Palace bildet den östlichen Abschluss an der nördlichen Seepromenade und prägt bis heute sowohl die Bebauung an der Haldenstrasse als auch das Stadtbild in seiner Fernwirkung. Der monumentale Hotelbau repräsentiert gemäss Roland Flückiger sowohl in bautechnischer als auch in gestalterischer Hinsicht den Höhepunkt der Schweizer Hotellerie ihrer Zeit. Während der Baukörper sich noch nach traditionellen Architekturformen richtet, lassen sich im Detail bereits Abweichungen wie die fehlende strikte Symmetrie erkennen. So gehört gemäss Flückiger das Palace durch die formale Abwandlung des traditionellen historischen Formengutes in Grund-

A TOUCH OF THE BELLE ÉPOQUE RETURNS

Cony Grünenfelder

REFURBISHING A MONUMENT

My first conversation with the client and the architect took place in the Hotel Palace's "Marlin" restaurant in 2015. Along the lakeside promenade, it seemed to me as if the exterior had remained largely unchanged and intact. After arriving at the hotel, I entered the building through today's main entrance on the west side and walked down the long corridor until I reached the spacious entrance hall. There was no indication where the restaurant was, so I walked through all the ground-floor rooms I could find along the showcase, lakeside façade, until I eventually returned to my starting point. Then a member of the hotel's staff led me to the restaurant. The experience was indicative of the situation of the hotel's ground floor before its refurbishment. The sequence of rooms was confusing and the individual salons were obscured. Archive research by the architect Iwan Bühler later confirmed my first impression: since the hotel had opened in 1906, the publicly accessible ground-floor rooms had undergone several structural changes and conversions at regular intervals, often taking no notice of the quality of the original fittings' design and craftsmanship. Due to this gradual process of sanitization over the years, the rooms not only lost their historical surfaces, but also their character. Based on a historical structural analysis, we agreed in initial discussions that the surviving historical traces in the publicly accessible ground-floor spaces should be exposed and made visible, thereby allowing a touch of the Belle Époche to re-emerge.

MONUMENT-PRESERVATION CONCEPT

The Hotel Palace forms the eastern conclusion of the northern lakeside promenade, and to this day can be seen from afar, dominating both the developments along Haldenstrasse and the cityscape. According to Roland Flückiger, the monumental hotel building represents the pinnacle of Swiss hotel development at the time, both in terms of structural engineering and with respect to its design. While the volume is still guided by traditional architectural forms, details such as a lack of a strict symmetry are indications of a deviating stance. Flückiger believes the formal modification of traditional, historical forms on the floor plan and façades makes the Palace one of the most important turn-of-the-century monuments in Lucerne.[1] Accordingly, the hotel is listed in the Swiss inventory of buildings most worthy of preservation, the ISOS, affording it the highest preservation status, while also recording its location as a local preservation zone. Since 2021, the hotel's preservation status has also been recorded in the land register and is binding for its owners.

The maintenance and heritage-preservation handling of the hotel's exterior was universally ac-

Blick in den Korridor, 1906
View down the corridor, 1906

Blick in den Korridor, 2016
View down the corridor, 2016

Blick in den Korridor, 2022
View down the corridor, 2022

riss und Fassade zu den bedeutendsten Luzerner Monumentalbauten der Jahrhundertwende. Entsprechend ist der Bau im ISOS – Inventar der schützenswerten Ortsbilder der Schweiz als Einzelobjekt mit dem höchsten Erhaltungsziel belegt und befindet sich ausserdem in der Ortsbildschutzzone. Seit 2021 ist der Schutzstatus auch eigentümerverbindlich im Grundbuch eingetragen.

Der Erhalt und denkmalpflegerische Umgang mit dem Äussern des Hotelbaus war von Beginn weg unbestritten. Hingegen war anfangs unklar, wie weit im Innern ein denkmalpflegerischer Umgang noch durch historische Substanz gerechtfertigt war. In mehreren Untersuchungsetappen wurden die historische Materialisierung und die Farbgebung am Äussern und im Innern durch die Restauratorin Liselotte Wechsler ermittelt.

Anhand dieser Untersuchungen, zahlreicher Sondagen sowie vertiefter Archivrecherchen erfassten die Architekten den Bestand in einem Raumbuch. Dieses machte deutlich, dass im Erdgeschoss sowie im Haupttreppenhaus unter zahlreichen Schichten noch historische Substanz vorhanden war. Aufgrund dieser Befundlage wurden Schutzziele für die öffentlich zugänglichen ehemaligen Repräsentationsräume im Erdgeschoss und für das Haupttreppenhaus formuliert. Gemeinsam verständigten sich Bauherrschaft, Architekt und Denkmalpflege auf den Erhalt und die Instandsetzung der noch vorhandenen historischen Bausubstanz.

Die Erneuerungsstrategie umfasste insbesondere Massnahmen, welche den historischen Charakter und die Wirkung der Räume im Erdgeschoss wieder stärken sollten, aber auch solche wie das Ordnen der Erdgeschossräume zur Verbesserung der Orientierung. Das Raumbuch und die restauratorischen Untersuchungen bildeten die Basis für die denkmalpflegerischen Massnahmen im Einzelnen. Unter Berücksichtigung der vorgefundenen historischen Bausubstanz und der vorhandenen räumlichen Qualitäten liessen sich die Räume in zwei Gruppen kategorisieren: einerseits in Räume mit bauzeitlicher Bausubstanz, deren historische Architekturoberflächen und -fassungen zu konservieren und restaurieren waren, und andererseits in Räume ohne relevante historische Bausubstanz, die neu interpretiert und gestaltet werden sollten. Zudem wurden Räume oder Raumteile benannt, welche nur teilweise über historische Architekturoberflächen verfügen, die in der bauzeitlichen Konzeption ergänzt und komplettiert werden sollten.

cepted from the outset. By contrast, it was initially unclear how far preservation work was justified indoors in view of the amount of surviving original fabric. In several analysis stages, the restorer Liselotte Wechsler carried out an assessment of the historical materialisation and colour scheme, both for the exterior and interior.

The architects managed to record the existing structure in a room book based on these studies, as well as numerous samples and in-depth archive research.[2] They underlined that both on the ground floor and at the main staircase, the historical fabric still existed beneath numerous other layers. These findings led to the formulation of preservation goals for the publicly accessible, formerly prestigious salons on the ground floor and the main staircase. Together with experts, the client, architect and preservation authority agreed on the conservation and renovation of the remaining historical building fabric.

The renovation strategy especially included measures to strengthen the historical character and effect of the salons on the ground floor, as well as other aspects such as the order of the ground-floor rooms to improve orientation. The room book and the restoration studies formed the basis of individual preservation measures. Taking the existing historical building fabric into account as well as spatial qualities, the salons could be categorised into two groups: those with historical building fabric, requiring the preservation and restoration of historical architectural surfaces and fittings, and secondly those without relevant historical building fabric, which could be reinterpreted and newly designed. Furthermore, rooms and parts of rooms were named where historical architectural surfaces had only partially survived, requiring supplementation and completion in accordance with the original concept.

Damensaal, Restaurierungsarbeiten am Stuck, 2022
Ladies' salon, restoration work on the stucco, 2022

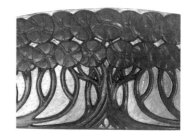

Damensaal, bauzeitliche Jugendstil-Dekoration, 2022
Ladies' salon, original art nouveau decoration, 2022

Damensaal, Sondage Verspiegelung, 2021
Ladies' salon, mirror analysis, 2021

Damensaal, 2022
Ladies' salon, 2022

Damensaal, Fotografie coloriert, 1906
Ladies' salon, coloured photograph, 1906

DAS INNERE

In mehreren Schritten untersuchte die Restauratorin Liselotte Wechsler, teilweise in einer Arbeitsgemeinschaft mit Wendel Odermatt, die historische Materialisierung und Farbgebung im Innern. Das Resultat präsentierte sich als ein vom Architekten Armin Meili-Wapf äusserst durchdachtes und stimmiges Material- und Farbkonzept, das sich durch das gesamte Gebäude zog. Die von Liselotte Wechsler als «mediterran sommerlich» bezeichnete historische Farbpalette präsentierte sich in unterschiedlicher Materialisierung:

Stuckmarmorflächen, die farblich von warmen, rötlichen und gelblichen bis hin zu grünlichen Tönen reichen, daneben Pinsel-Marmorierung in verschiedenen Grün-Nuancen, Marmor in weisser, grauen und schwarzer Farbe sowie durch Stuck gegliederte Wand- und Deckenflächen; das Ganze zusammengebunden durch einen dunklen Sockel – teilweise als Stuckmarmorierung, teilweise als Pinselmarmorierung oder als Gotthard-Serpentin in Naturstein –, der sich als Band durch sämtliche Räume zog und den Übergang zwischen Boden und Wandflächen akzentuierte.

DAS ERDGESCHOSS

Ursprünglich waren die repräsentativen Gesellschaftsräume im Erdgeschoss als klare Raumabfolge konzipiert. Ausgehend von der zentralen Eingangshalle erschlossen sich gegen Osten das Restaurant sowie der Speisesaal. Gegen Westen fügten sich Lesesaal, Damensaal, Musiksaal und Bar aneinander. Eine vorgelagerte Veranda sowie der rückwärtige Korridor ermöglichten ein vielfältiges Durch- und Umschreiten der verschiedenen Raumschichten der Repräsentationsräume. Die 2015 vorgefundene Unübersichtlichkeit im Erdgeschoss hatte zwei Gründe: Einerseits hatten zahlreiche Umbauten im Laufe der letzten hundert Jahre die ursprüngliche Struktur verbaut und den bauzeitlichen Raumschmuck sowie die historischen Oberflächen bis auf Restbestände reduziert oder zerstört. Andererseits hatte die Verlegung des Haupteingangs Ende der 1980er-Jahre von der Haldenstrasse an die Westseite die im Erdgeschoss-Grundriss ursprünglich angelegte klare Raumabfolge der repräsentativen Gesellschaftsräume und die damit verbundene Dramaturgie aufgelöst. Der ursprünglich axial angelegte Haupteingang führte in die zentrale Eingangshalle und ermöglichte den Gästen eine klare Orientierung im Gebäude. Da er sich nicht wieder an seinen bauzeitlichen Standort zurückverlegen liess, musste die Raumabfolge neu überdacht werden. So kam die Rezeption möglichst nahe an den heutigen Haupteingang in die westliche Gebäudeecke und ans Ende der Raumabfolge zu liegen, dort, wo sich zur Bauzeit der Musiksaal befand. Da von der historischen Ausstattung und

THE INTERIOR

In several stages, the restorer Liselotte Wechsler investigated the interior's historical materialisation and colour scheme, partly in collaboration with Wendel Odermatt. The result turned out to be a harmonious material and colour concept that was extremely well thought through by the architect Armin Meili-Wapf, running through the entire building. Described by Liselotte Wechsler as "like a Mediterranean summer",[3] the range of colours is expressed in various materials: stucco-marble surfaces in colours ranging from warm, reddish and yellow hues to greenish tones, including brush-painted marble effects in various grey nuances, marble in white, grey and black colours, as well as wall and ceiling surfaces structured by stucco; all bound together by a dark base – partly as marble-patterned stucco, partly as brush-painted marble patterns or in natural Gotthard-Serpentinite stone, which ran in a band around all rooms and accentuated the transition between the floor and the walls.

THE GROUND FLOOR

Originally, the official social rooms were arranged on the ground floor in a clear spatial sequence. Starting with the central entrance hall, the restaurant and dining hall were accessed to the east, while towards the west, the reading, ladies' salon, music room and bar adjoined with one another. A veranda in front of the rooms and a rear corridor allowed diverse mobility through and between the different spatial layers of the social rooms. The confusing arrangement on the ground floor that was found in 2015 had two reasons: firstly, numerous conversions over the last 100 years had obstructed the original structure, reducing or even destroying the original structures and room ornamentation, while eradicating the historical surfaces apart from a few remnants. Secondly, the main entrance was moved from Haldenstrasse to the west side of the building in the late 1980s, thereby breaking down the originally clear spatial sequence of prestigious social rooms and destroying the narrative connected to it. The original, axial main entrance led to the central entrance hall and provided clear orientation for all guests. Since it could not be repositioned to its original place, the spatial sequence had to be reconsidered. Thus the reception came as close to today's main entrance as possible, in the western corner of the building, at the end of the spatial sequence, where the music room had originally been located. Since no traces of the historical decoration and architectural surfaces, as seen on coloured photos dating back to 1906, could be found, the room could be reinterpreted and newly designed.

In the ground-floor corridor, which had by now lost all of its original ornamentation, pilasters and round arches were reinstalled on the walls and ceilings in a reduced architectural language. The measure is inspired by the original spatial effect, picking up on the structure of the long corridor. The doors providing access to the main rooms on the lake side are just as important for the structure. They were pro-

den Architekturoberflächen, wie sie auf dem kolorierten Foto von 1906 zu sehen sind, keine Spuren mehr zu finden waren, konnte dieser Raum neu interpretiert und gestaltet werden.

Im Erdgeschoss-Korridor, dem mittlerweile jeglicher Bauschmuck abhanden gekommen war, wurden in einer reduzierten Architektursprache wieder Pilaster und Rundbogen an Wänden und Decke aufgesetzt. Diese Massnahme lehnt sich lediglich an die ursprüngliche Raumwirkung an und greift die Gliederung des langen Korridors wieder auf. Ebenso wichtig für die Gliederung sind auch die Türen, welche die seeseitigen Haupträume erschliessen. Sie wurden in Nussbaumholz mit Messingbeschlägen ausgeführt. Beide Eingriffe sind als neue Interventionen klar ablesbar, fügen sich aber ganz selbstverständlich ein. Die neuen Leuchter referenzieren in ihrer Materialität auf historische Aufnahmen, ohne jedoch eine historisierende Formensprache zu übernehmen.

Trotz einiger im Laufe der Zeit erfolgter Veränderungen war im ehemaligen Damensaal noch viel historische Substanz vorhanden. Der auf einem kolorierten Foto von 1906 abgebildete Raum unterschied sich lediglich in wenigen Punkten von der angetroffenen Raumsituation. Die rote Stoffbespannung und das Cheminée waren längst verschwunden. Fotos belegen, dass in den 1960er-Jahren der Damensaal stark purifiziert worden war. Das heisst, der von uns vorgefundene Zustand, der sehr viele Übereinstimmungen mit der historischen Aufnahme von 1906 hatte, war bereits wieder eine Annäherung und teilweise Wiederherstellung. Zwar hatte die reich verzierte Stuckdecke durch mehrere dicke Farbschichten ihre plastische Wirkung verloren, aber sie war vollständig erhalten geblieben. Die Wandflächen waren zwar noch durch vergoldete Stuckrahmen gegliedert, doch die einzelnen Wandfelder und Wandöffnungen hatten sich stark verändert. Nach dem Entfernen mehrerer kunststoffvergüteter Farbschichten wurde die Stuckdecke freigelegt und nach Befund neu gefasst: Die Deckenflächen in einem dunkleren und die Erhöhungen der Stuckprofile in einem helleren Gelbton; dazu kommen einzelne vergoldete Dekorelemente. Bei Sondagen kamen die bauzeitlichen verspiegelten Holzeinbauten, welche bei zwei Türnischen vorgeblendet waren, zum Vorschein. Selbst die florale Jugendstilverzierung auf dem Kämpfer hatte sich erhalten. Die ursprünglichen Wandfelder und -öffnungen konnten wiederhergestellt und die Stuckrahmen der Wandfelder restauriert werden. Nach dem Wegfall der dicken Farbpakete auf Stuckdecke und Stuckrahmen sind die Dekorationselemente wieder lesbar. Dabei überrascht das vorgefundene direkte Nebeneinander – das nicht einer eher erwarteten Verschmelzung entspricht – der klassizistischen Stilelemente von Decke und Wandflächen und der verspielten Stil-

duced in walnut wood with brass fittings. Both measures are clearly legible as new interventions, but are nevertheless naturally integrated into the existing structure. The new chandelier's materiality is based on historical photographs, without assuming a historicising formal language.

Despite a number of changes over the years, much of the former ladies' salon's original building fabric still existed. The room, which was recorded on a coloured photograph dated 1906, differed only slightly from the encountered spatial situation. The red textile covering and the cheminée had long disappeared. Photos reveal that in the 1960s, the ladies' salon was strongly simplified. Thus, the condition in which we found it had very many consistencies with the historical photograph of 1906 and was already an approximation and partial reconstruction.[4] Although the richly decorated stucco ceiling had lost its sculptural effect due to several thick layers of paint, it had remained completely preserved. The wall surfaces were still structured by gold-leaf stucco frames, but the individual wall areas and apertures had been considerably changed. After removing several polymer-modified layers of paint, the stucco ceiling was exposed and repainted according to the discovered original tone: the ceiling areas in a darker yellow and the heightened stucco profiles in a lighter yellow tone; these were supplemented with individual gold-leaf décor elements. Probing revealed the original mirrored wooden fittings behind casing on two door niches. Even the floral art nouveau ornamentation has remained preserved. The original wall panels and apertures could be reconstructed and the wall areas' stucco frames restored. After removing the thick colour layers on the stucco ceiling and stucco frames, the decorative elements became legible again. The discovered direct juxtaposition is surprising – as opposed to the expected merging – of neoclassicist style elements on the ceiling and wall surfaces, as well as the playful style elements of neoclassicism on the mirroring, and the art nouveau in the former ladies' salon.

For the textile covering on the wall surfaces, a gold-stitched fabric was developed and produced in collaboration with the textile expert Birgit Roller (see p. 92). It firstly picks up on the lily motif used in the hotel, while secondly referring to the originally used Jacquard materials. The marble edging on the wall apertures and the dark green marble-patterned wooden base were preserved. The painstakingly restored room details on the walls and ceilings were supplemented with new walnut wooden doors, a dark parquet and a colour-coordinated fitted milieu-carpet.

THE MAIN STAIRCASE

The greatest surprise was revealed at the staircase. Beneath polymer-modified paint, the original stucco-marble was still preserved, while the historical terrazzo slabs were discovered beneath the fitted carpet. Wherever possible, the stucco-marble was exposed and restored, although it had to be supplemented in some areas. Following the renovation measures, the

elemente des Jugendstils auf den verspiegelten Türöffnungen im ehemaligen Damensaal.

Für die Stoffbespannung in den Wandfeldern wurde in Zusammenarbeit mit der Textilfachfrau Birgit Roller eine Goldstickerei entworfen und angefertigt (vgl. Text S. 92). Diese nimmt einerseits das im Hotel verwendete Motiv der Lilie auf und stellt zugleich den Bezug zu den bauzeitlich verwendeten Jacquard-Stoffen her. Die Marmoreinfassungen der Wandöffnung sowie der dunkelgrün marmorierte Holzsockel waren erhalten geblieben. Ergänzt wurde die sorgfältig restaurierte Raumausstattung von Wand und Decke mit neuen Holztüren aus Nussbaum, einem dunklen Parkett sowie einem farblich eingepassten Milieu-Teppich.

DAS HAUPTTREPPENHAUS

Die grösste Überraschung gab es im Treppenhaus zu entdecken. Unter kunststoffhaltigen Anstrichen verbarg sich noch immer der bauzeitliche Stuckmarmor, und unter den Spannteppichen kamen die historischen Terrazzo-Platten zum Vorschein. Dort, wo es möglich war, wurde der Stuckmarmor freigelegt und restauriert. An einigen Stellen musste er ergänzt werden. Nach der Renovation präsentiert sich das Treppenhaus wieder in seiner bauzeitlichen Gestaltung: Wände, die mit einem Stuckprofil in einen unteren Teil mit Stuckmarmor und einen oberen Teil mit einer glatten Fläche gegliedert sind. Das bauzeitliche Treppengeländer aus Metall zeigt sich wieder in einem dunklen Grünton, wobei die punktuellen Dekorelemente, die bauzeitlich in Messing gefertigt waren und später bronziert wurden, nicht freigelegt werden konnten. Hingegen wurden die Farbanstriche auf dem hölzernen Handlauf wieder entfernt. Auch die Terrazzo-Platten auf den Treppenpodesten und in den Geschoss-Korridoren konnten freigelegt und geschliffen werden. So sind es die historischen Architekturoberflächen, die dem Treppenhaus wieder einen denkmalwürdigen Auftritt geben.

DAS ÄUSSERE

Auf den ersten Blick hat sich das Hotel Palace in seinem äusseren Erscheinungsbild seit seiner Erbauung wenig verändert. Auf den zweiten Blick wird erkennbar, dass über die Jahrzehnte doch zahlreiche kleinere und grössere Eingriffe erfolgten.

DAS DACH

Die grössten Veränderungen am Äusseren erfolgten im Dachbereich. Die erste wesentliche bauliche Anpassung geht zurück auf den 1967 eingebauten Personen- und Warenlift, der mit einem neuen massiven Aufbau auf dem Dach an der Nordseite verbunden war. Auf Fotoaufnahmen aus den 1970er-Jahren ist diese Liftüberfahrt als Betonkubus erkennbar. Durch die

staircase now presents itself in its original design: walls structured with a stucco profile on their lower sections, with stucco-marble and a smooth-surface upper section. The original banisters made of metal have regained their dark green tone, while the accentuating ornamental elements, which were originally made of brass and later bronze-plated, could not be exposed. By contrast, the paint layers on the wooden handrails were removed. The terrazzo slabs on the staircase landings and the corridors of each floor were exposed and polished. Thus the historical architectural surfaces have re-established the staircase's heritage status.

THE EXTERIOR

At first sight, the exterior appearance of the Hotel Palace seems to have changed little since its construction. On closer inspection however, it becomes apparent that over the decades, numerous smaller and more substantial interventions had been carried out.

THE ROOF

The greatest changes to the exterior were performed on the roof area. The first significant structural alteration dates back to 1967, with the installed staff and goods lift, which was combined with a new, massive structure on the roof's north side. Photographs from the 1970s show the projecting concrete cube at the top of the elevator hoistway. The conversion measures in the early 1990s, which covered the volume with tiles, only strengthened the impression that the top of the hoistway was a crude, oversized rooftop structure.

In the 1970s, there was a substantial dispute concerning the first project, which included heightening the hotel and completely replacing the roof. The Swiss monument preservation authority also got involved. The measures were described as a "coffin-lid solution" that would destroy the artistic synthesis of the Hotel Palace as a whole.[5] As a result, it took around 20 years, until 1993/94, before a general refurbishment was carried out, including a redesigned roof. It decisively altered the once harmonious roof landscape. The interventions included adding one floor to the building, as well as further rooms. The heightening measure greatly reduced the autonomous presence of the tower, the dome and the side avant-corps. Shifting the position of the elevator during current conversion measures made it possible to remove the oversized shaft structure on the roof. Originally, the client wanted to alter and enlarge the lucarnes on the attic level that had been created by the 1993 measures. However, as the project progressed, the owners changed their minds.

Haupttreppenhaus, 2022
Main staircase, 2022

Haupttreppenhaus, 1906
Main staircase, 1906

Haupttreppenhaus, 2016
Main staircase, 2016

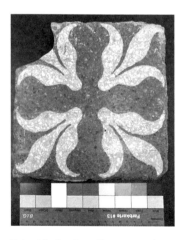

Befund Bodenplatte Haupttreppenhaus, 2018
Floor plate findings, main staircase, 2018

anfangs der 1990er-Jahre ausgeführte Umgestaltung, bei der das Volumen mit Ziegeln eingedeckt wurde, verstärkte sich der Eindruck der Überfahrt als plumper und überproportionierter Dachaufsatz.

In den 1970er-Jahren gab es eine heftige Auseinandersetzung um das erste Projekt, das eine Aufstockung und den kompletten Ersatz des Daches beinhaltete, in die sich auch der Schweizerische Heimatschutz einschaltete. Es war die Rede von einer «Sargdeckellösung», welche die Einheit des Gesamtkunstwerkes «Hotel Palace» zerstöre. In der Folge dauerte es rund zwanzig Jahre, bis 1993/94 eine Total-Erneuerung und Umgestaltung des Dachs erfolgte. Sie veränderte die einst harmonische Dachlandschaft einschneidend. Damals wurde ein zusätzliches Geschoss eingeführt und weitere Zimmer realisiert. Durch diese Aufstockung reduzierte sich die eigenständige Präsenz von Turm, Kuppel und Seitenrisaliten in ihrer Wirkung stark. Durch das Verschieben der Liftanlage im Rahmen des jetzigen Umbaus konnte der überdimensionierte Aufbau wieder rückgebaut werden. Anfänglich sollten gemäss dem Wunsch der Bauherrschaft die Lukarnen im 1993 entstandenen zweiten Dachgeschoss verändert und vergrössert werden. Im Laufe des Projekts liess die Eigentümerschaft diese Absicht jedoch fallen.

FASSADE

Die Fassaden des Hotel Palace sind geprägt durch das Wechselspiel zwischen verputzten Fassadenflächen und plastischem Fassadenschmuck in Natur- und Kunststein. Der Vergleich von Fotografien liess vermuten, dass sich die Fassaden seit der Bauzeit im Wesentlichen erhalten hatten. Der restauratorische Farbuntersuch bestätigte eine Farbigkeit der Fassade, die im Grossen und Ganzen nach wie vor dem bauzeitlichen Konzept entsprach. Der historische Verputz wurde vermutlich 1984 bei einer Fassadenrenovation durch einen armierten, kunststoffhaltigen Fassadenverputz ersetzt. Dieser präsentierte sich in einem intakten Zustand, sodass er belassen werden musste. Aus ästhetischen Gründen konnte er lediglich leicht abgeglättet werden: Die grobe Struktur wurde mit dem Auftrag einer feinen Putzschicht der bauzeitlichen Putzstruktur angepasst. Es kam ein eingefärbter Verputz zum Einsatz, welcher die ursprüngliche Farbigkeit noch präzisiert, die an einzelnen Stellen, so zum Beispiel bei der Demontage der Balkongeländer, zum Vorschein kam. Die historischen Balkongeländer – 2007/08 bereits in ihrer Höhe angepasst – wurden mit zusätzlichen Dekorelementen ergänzt, damit auch die Zwischenräume und Abstände der Einzelteile den Normanforderungen entsprechen. Schlussendlich wurden sie in einem dunklen Grünton gefasst.

FAÇADE

The Hotel Palace façades are characterised by an interplay between plastered façade areas and sculptural façade ornamentation in natural and artificial stone. A comparison of photographs led to the suspicion that the façade had been largely preserved since its original construction. The restoration colour analysis[6] confirmed a colour scheme for the façade that was very similar to the concept implemented at the time of the building's construction. The historical plaster was presumably replaced in 1984 with a reinforced, polymer-modified façade plaster. It was intact and therefore had to be preserved. For aesthetic reasons, it was simply smoothed over: the coarse structure was adapted by applying a fine layer of plaster to resemble the plaster at the time of construction. Elsewhere, a dyed plaster was used that even reflects the original colour scheme, which was occasionally revealed, for instance when dismantling the balcony railings. The historical balcony railings – with altered heights following measures in 2007/08 – were supplemented with additional decorative elements so that the interstices and distances between individual elements also conformed to the required standard. Finally, they were painted dark green.

The windows from the original construction period, with their curved imposts on the fourth floor, which are still visible on photographs from 1974, had unfortunately long been replaced. New windows can be seen on photos from 1977. Today's wooden and metal windows on the upper levels – which were installed in stages from 2005 onwards – do not conform to monument preservation guidelines due to their materialisation and profile, but could not (yet) be replaced due to a grandfathering clause, since they had not yet outlived their service lifespan. Wherever windows needed to be replaced, they were designed in accordance with the original partitions and profiles used at the time of the building's construction. This was particularly the case with the windows on the base level. These wooden windows set the standard for future window replacements on the entire building. The large sliding windows on the prestigious ground-floor rooms, affording views of the lake, received their original divisions with curved imposts and an exterior light-grey colour. This window colour scheme was shown to have existed both on a highlight-window on the large dome and on a small oriel window that had survived.[7]

CONCLUSION

The Hotel Palace with its characteristic roof landscape has regained its important presence in the cityscape of Lucerne. Attractive, publicly accessible spaces have been created on the ground floor, which are naturally integrated into the historical structures, reviving the Belle Époque atmosphere.

The conversion of the Hotel Palace is a refurbishment based on preservation measures, rather than a general restoration. Only a small part of the imple-

Die Fenster aus der Bauzeit mit ihren geschwungenen Kämpfern im vierten Obergeschoss, auf Fotos aus 1974 noch erkennbar, waren leider längst ersetzt. Bereits auf Fotos von 1977 sind neue Fenster abgebildet. Die heutigen Holzmetall-Fenster in den Obergeschossen – ab 2005 in Etappen ausgeführt – genügen aufgrund ihrer Materialisierung und Profilierung denkmalpflegerischen Anforderungen nicht, konnten aber leider aufgrund der Bestandesgarantie (noch) nicht ersetzt werden, da ihre Lebensdauer noch nicht abgelaufen ist. Dort, wo jedoch Fenster erneuert werden mussten, sind sie in Anlehnung an die Bauzeit mit der entsprechenden Einteilung und Profilierung gestaltet worden. Das war insbesondere bei der Befensterung des Sockelgeschosses der Fall. Diese Holzfenster geben den Massstab für künftige Fenstererneuerungen am gesamten Gebäude vor. Die grossen Schiebefenster in den repräsentativen Erdgeschossräumen, welche den Blick auf den See freigeben, erhielten die ursprüngliche Fensterteilung mit dem geschwungenen Kämpfer und sind aussen in einem hellen Grauton gefasst. Diese Farbfassung der Fenster konnte nachgewiesen werden, sowohl an einem Fenster in der Laterne der grossen Kuppel als auch bei einem kleinen Erkerfenster, das erhalten geblieben ist.

FAZIT

Das Hotel Palace mit seiner charakteristischen Dachlandschaft hat seine gewichtige Präsenz im Stadtbild von Luzern zurückgewonnen. Im Erdgeschoss sind attraktive, öffentlich zugängliche Räume entstanden, die sich selbstverständlich in den historischen Bestand einfügen und die Belle Époque wieder spürbar machen.

Beim erfolgten Umbau des Hotels Palace handelt es sich um eine denkmalpflegerische Erneuerung, nicht um eine Gesamtrestaurierung. Nur ein kleiner Teil der umgesetzten baulichen Massnahmen erfolgte in einem engeren restauratorischen Sinn, indem historische Oberflächen instand gestellt, konserviert und ergänzt wurden. Diese beschränkten sich im Wesentlichen auf den ehemaligen Damensaal sowie auf das Haupttreppenhaus. Trotzdem ist jenseits von denkmalpflegerischen Idealvorstellungen ein grosser Mehrwert entstanden, denn heute ist das Hotel Palace auch im Innern wieder als historisches Hotel wahrnehmbar. Das Ringen um Lösungen, welche die Vereinbarkeit mit dem Denkmalwert in den Fokus stellten, hat sich gelohnt. Der Architekt Iwan Bühler und sein Team haben mit gebührendem Respekt vor der noch vorhandenen historischen Bausubstanz und dem bauzeitlichen Farb- und Materialkonzept ein differenziertes Erneuerungskonzept entwickelt, welches eine Vielzahl von Ansprüchen zu integrieren vermochte: Sehr hohe Komfortansprüche eines Fünf-Sterne-

Ansicht von Westen, um 1910
View from the west, around 1910

mented structural measures were carried out in the strict sense of restoration, which repairs, preserves and supplements historical surfaces. Such measures were largely limited to the former ladies' salon and the main staircase. Nevertheless, a great added value has been achieved, going beyond monument-preservation ideals, since today, the Hotel Palace can also be experienced as a historical hotel from the inside. Efforts to find solutions that focused on harmonising with the building's value as a monument have paid off. The architect Iwan Bühler and his team have developed a differentiated renewal concept with appropriate respect for the still surviving historical building fabric, as well as the original colour and material concept, which managed to integrate a great variety of demands: the very high comfort levels of a five-star hotel, today's fire-safety and security standards, as well as adaptations for the latest building technology, all had to be accommodated.

They fulfilled these demands not with contrasting interventions, but by skilfully continuing the historical canon of materials and colours, while supplementing historical elements with new aspects to create a coherent unity. Rooms where no historical substance had survived were redesigned. The entrance hall – today's bar – has once again become the actual heart of the hotel, its original spatial effect expertly translated and reinterpreted. The former ladies' salon was restored, while missing fittings were supplemented with newly designed elements such as the textile wall covering, the parquet and the milieu carpet. The result is a magnificent salon that impresses with its well-balanced atmosphere.

Hotels, heutige Anforderungen an Brandschutz und Sicherheit sowie Anpassungen an die neueste Gebäudetechnik waren zu verkraften.

Sie lösten diese Erfordernisse nicht mit kontrastreichen Eingriffen, sondern mit dem gekonnten Fortführen des historischen Material- und Farbkanons, ergänzten das Historische mit Neuem zu einer stimmigen Gesamtheit. Räume, in denen keine historische Substanz mehr vorhanden war, wurden neu gestaltet. Die Eingangshalle – heute Bar – ist wieder zum eigentlichen Herzstück des Hotels geworden. Die ursprüngliche Raumwirkung wurde gekonnt übersetzt und interpretiert. Der ehemalige Damensaal wurde restauriert, die fehlenden Ausstattungsteile mit neu gestalteten Elementen wie der Stoffbespannung, dem Parkett und dem Milieu-Teppich ergänzt. Entstanden ist ein prächtiger Saal, der mit seiner ausgewogenen Stimmung zu überzeugen vermag.

Insgesamt konnte der Denkmalwert dieses wichtigen Zeugen der Luzerner Hotel- und Tourismusgeschichte gestärkt werden. Der historische Farb- und Materialklang prägt heute wieder die ehemaligen Repräsentationsräume im Erdgeschoss und sind so als Zeugnisse der Belle Époque wieder erlebbar.

Overall, the heritage value of this important example of Lucerne's hotel and tourist history has been enhanced. Today, the historical colour and material tones once again characterise the former society rooms on the ground floor, allowing them to be enjoyed as vestiges of the Belle Époque.

1 Roland Flückiger-Seiler, *Hotel Palace. Hotel- und Tourismusinventar*, 1998.
2 Iwan Bühler, *Hotel Palace, Raumbuch, 1906 und 2016*
3 Liselotte Wechsler, *Hotel Palace. Historischer Befund. Farbe und Material, 2. Etappe*, 2019.
4 Liselotte Wechsler, *Hotel Palace, Abbildungskatalog Innen*, 2018.
5 Robert Steiner, letter by the Swiss Monument Preservation Authority (Schweizer Heimatschutz) to Dr. Otto Meyer, President of the Administrative Board, Hotel Palace AG, dated March 8, 1973.
6 Liselotte Wechsler, *Hotel Palace. Farbgebung in Anlehnung an die Bauzeit – Fassaden, Befundaufnahme und Farbtonermittlung*, 2020.
7 Liselotte Wechsler, *Hotel Palace. Abbildungskatalog Aussen*, 2018.

1 Roland Flückiger-Seiler, *Hotel Palace. Hotel- und Tourismusinventar*, 1998.
2 Iwan Bühler, *Hotel Palace, Raumbuch*, 1906 und 2016.
3 Liselotte Wechsler, *Hotel Palace. Historischer Befund. Farbe und Material, 2. Etappe*, 2019.
4 Liselotte Wechsler, *Hotel Palace, Abbildungskatalog Innen*, 2018.
5 Robert Steiner, Schreiben Schweizer Heimatschutz an Dr. Otto Meyer, Präsident des Verwaltungsrates der Hotel Palace AG vom 8. März 1973.
6 Liselotte Wechsler, *Hotel Palace. Farbgebung in Anlehnung an die Bauzeit – Fassaden, Befundaufnahme und Farbtonermittlung*, 2020.
7 Liselotte Wechsler, *Hotel Palace. Abbildungskatalog Aussen*, 2018.

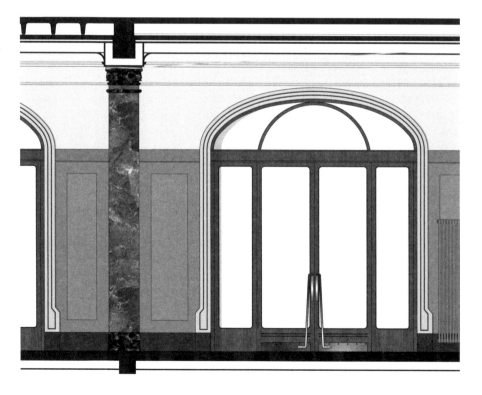

Halle, 1906, Architekt: Heinrich
Meili-Wapf,
Hall, 1906, architect: Heinrich Meili-Wapf

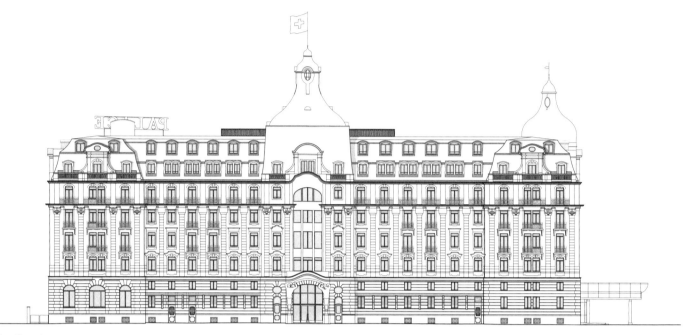

Nordfassade
North façade

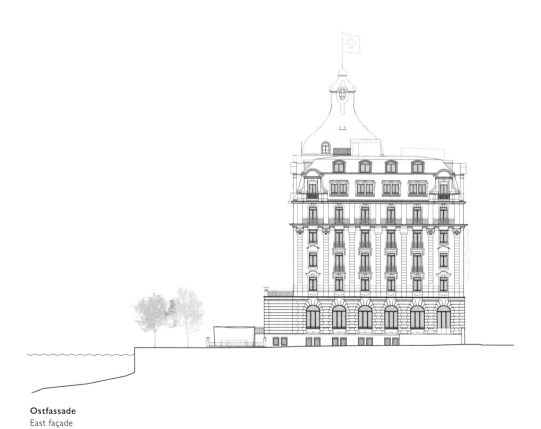

Ostfassade
East façade

10 m

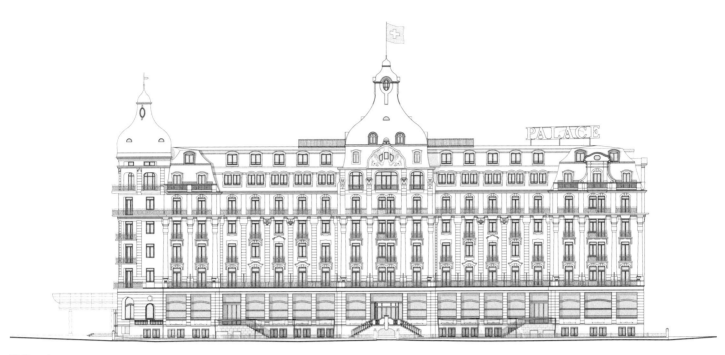

Südfassade
South façade

Westfassade
West façade

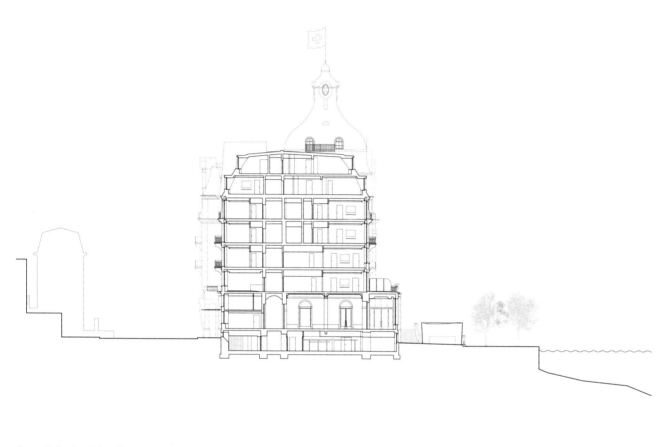

Querschnitt durch den Damensaal
Sectional view through the ladies' salon

10 m

Querschnitt durch die Halle/Haupttreppenhaus
Sectional view through the hall/main staircase

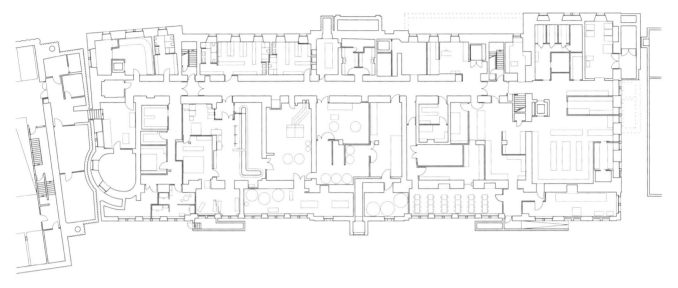

Untergeschoss
Basement

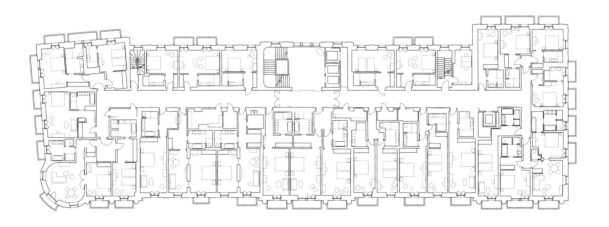

2. Obergeschoss
2nd floor

10 m

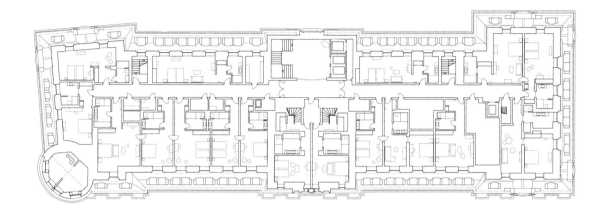

6. Obergeschoss
6th floor

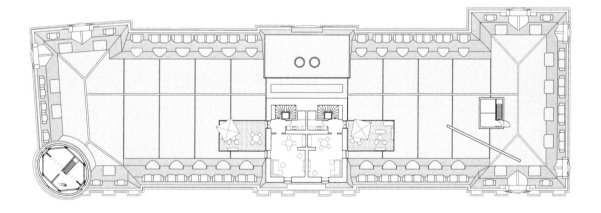

Dachgeschoss
Attic level

1 **Rezeption**
2 **Damensaal**
3 **Lesesaal, Kapo (Japanisches Restaurant)**
4 **Halle, Bar**
5 **Restaurant**
6 **Saal**
1 Reception
2 Ladies' salon
3 Reading room (Japanese restaurant)
4 Hall, bar
5 Restaurant
6 Hall

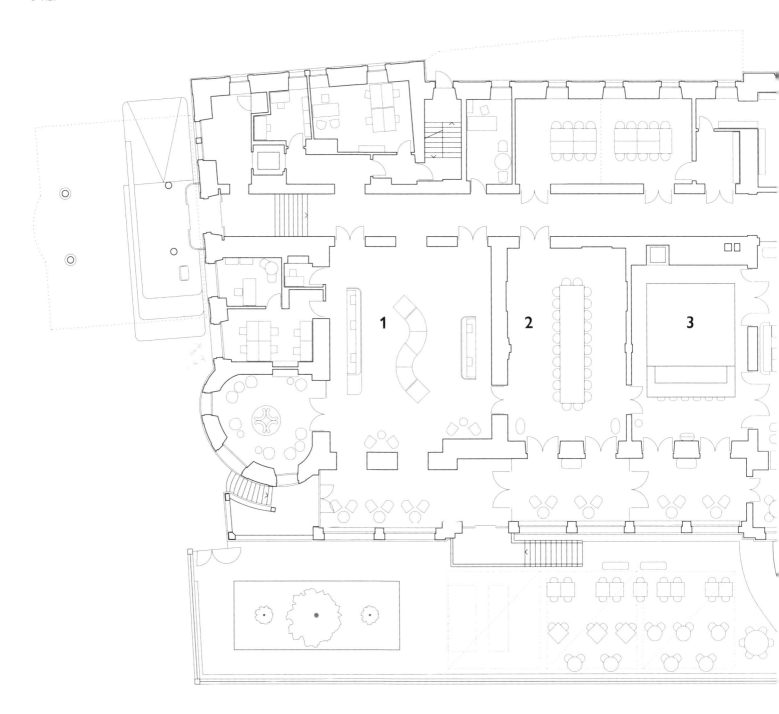

Erdgeschoss
Ground floor

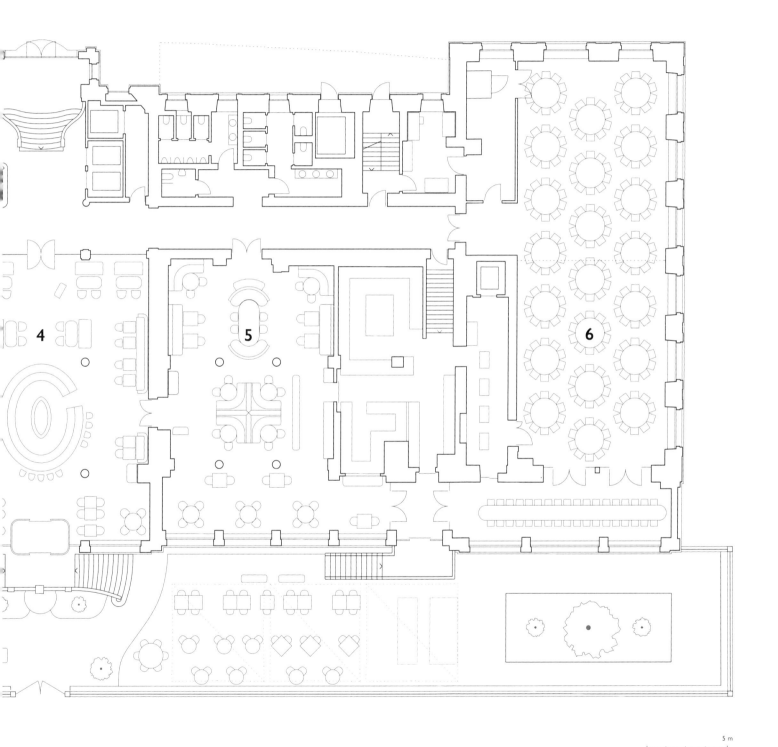

4

5

6

5 m

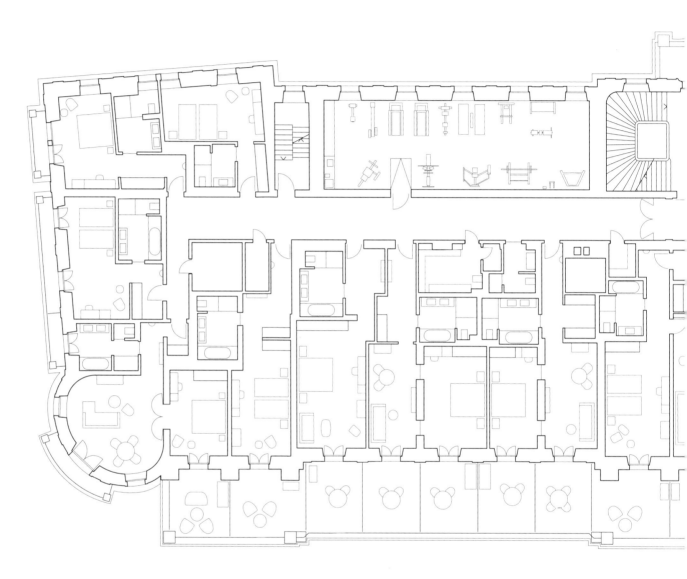

1. Obergeschoss
1st floor

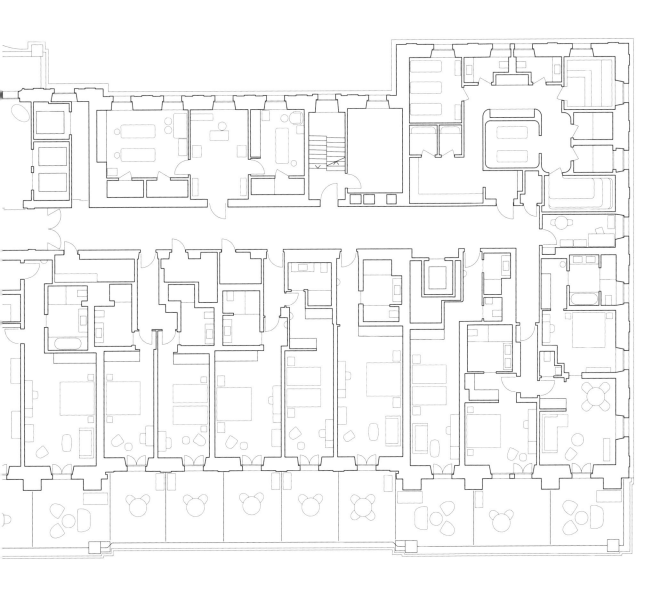

5 m

PROJEKTORGANISATION

BAUHERRSCHAFT
First Swiss Hotel Collection AG, Luzern

PROJEKTLEITUNG BAUHERR
Chengbin Miao, Lijun Yu

BETREIBER
Mandarin Oriental Hotel Group, Hongkong

ARCHITEKT
Iwan Bühler Architekten, Luzern
Projektleitung: Carmen Blum, Iwan Bühler, Marco De Donno, Louis Zoller
Mitarbeitende: Anne-Katrin Brandau, Chantal Bussmann, Marc Coll, Thomas Filzer, Raphael Koller, Ane Lang, Svenja Locher, Christina Luckhardt, Philipp Mächler, Christa Marti, Luca Sennhauser, Andrea Steiger, Ronal Veras

GENERALPLANUNG UND BAULEITUNG
Itten+Brechbühl AG, Zürich
Projektleitung: Franziska Willers, Kuno Zimmermann
Mitarbeitende: Pascal Beske, Sara Conde, Martin Dahinden, Raquel Gomez Sanchez, Joe Kaps, Holger Meissner, Cedomir Nikolic, Alexandra Pongratz, Nicolas Steiner, René Walder, Daniel Zwimpfer

TRAGWERKSPLANUNG
WAM Planer und Ingenieure AG, Bern

ELEKTROPLANUNG
PZM Luzern AG, Horw

HLKS-PLANUNG
W&P Engineering AG, Stansstad

LICHTPLANUNG
LICHTTEAM AG, Rothenburg

LANDSCHAFTSARCHITEKTUR
SKK Landschaftsarchitekten AG, Wettingen

INNENARCHITEKTUR
Jestico + Whiles, London

KUNSTKONZEPTION
VISTO, Paris/Nicosia

BAUPHYSIK
Kopitsis Bauphysik AG, Wohlen

FOTOGRAF
Ruedi Walti Fotografie, Basel

BRANDSCHUTZPLANUNG
tib Technik im Bau AG, Luzern

BAUTERMINE (CHRONOLOGIE)
Planungsbeginn: 2015
Baubewilligung: 2017
Baubeginn: Oktober 2018
Fertigstellung: August 2022
Feierliche Eröffnung: 24. September 2022

RESTAURATORIN/FARBANALYSEN
ARGE Liselotte Wechsler, Luzern,
& Stöckli AG, Stans

KÜCHENPLANUNG
Simeta AG, Niederwil

SIGNALETIK
WBG AG – Visuelle Kommunikation, Zürich

TÜRFACHPLANUNG
HKG Consulting, Aarau

PROJECT ORGANISATION

CLIENT
First Swiss Hotel Collection AG, Lucerne

PROJECT MANAGEMENT (CLIENT)
Chengbin Miao, Lijun Yu

OPERATOR
Mandarin Oriental Hotel Group, Hong Kong

ARCHITECT
Iwan Bühler Architekten, Lucerne
Project management: Carmen Blum, Iwan Bühler, Marco De Donno, Louis Zoller
Team: Anne-Katrin Brandau, Chantal Bussmann, Marc Coll, Thomas Filzer, Raphael Koller, Ane Lang, Svenja Locher, Christina Luckhardt, Philipp Mächler, Christa Marti, Luca Sennhauser, Andrea Steiger, Ronal Veras

GENERAL PLANNING AND BUILDING MANAGEMENT
Itten+Brechbühl AG, Zurich
Project management: Franziska Willers, Kuno Zimmermann
Team: Pascal Beske, Sara Conde, Martin Dahinden, Raquel Gomez Sanchez, Joe Kaps, Holger Meissner, Cedomir Nikolic, Alexandra Pongratz, Nicolas Steiner, René Walder, Daniel Zwimpfer

STRUCTURAL ENGINEER
WAM Planer und Ingenieure AG, Bern

ELECTRICAL ENGINEERING
PZM Luzern AG, Horw

HVACS ENGINEERING
W&P Engineering AG, Stansstad

LIGHTING PLANNING
LICHTTEAM AG, Rothenburg

LANDSCAPE ARCHITECTURE
SKK Landschaftsarchitekten AG, Wettingen

INTERIOR ARCHITECTURE
Jestico + Whiles, London

STRUCTURAL PHYSICIST
Kopitsis Bauphysik AG, Wohlen

FIRE-SAFETY PLANNING
tib Technik im Bau AG, Lucerne

RESTORER/ COLOUR ANALYSIS
ARGE Liselotte Wechsler, Lucerne,
& Stöckli AG, Stans

KITCHEN PLANNER
Simeta AG, Niederwil

SIGNAGE
WBG AG – Visuelle Kommunikation, Zurich

SPECIALIST DOOR PLANNER
HKG Consulting, Aarau

ART CONCEPT
VISTO, Paris/Nicosia

PHOTOGRAPHER
Ruedi Walti Fotografie, Basel

PROJECT CHRONOLOGY
Planning begun: 2015
Planning permission: 2017
Construction begun: October 2018
Completion: August 2022
Official opening: September 24, 2022

IWAN BÜHLER

1958	Geboren in Luzern
1987	Architekturdiplom an der ETH Zürich bei Prof. Dolf Schnebli
1988–1989	Mitarbeit im Architekturbüro Anton Bühlmann, Hergiswil
1990–1992	Assistent an der ETH Zürich bei Prof. André Corboz, Lehrstuhl für Städtebau
1990–	Eigenes Architekturbüro in Luzern

CONY GRÜNENFELDER (TEXTBEITRAG)

1963	Geboren in Luzern
1984	Lehrabschluss als Innenausbauzeichnerin
1993	Diplom als Architektin HTL, Zentralschweizerisches Technikum Luzern
1993–2004	Mitarbeit im Architekturbüro Iwan Bühler, Luzern
2004–2007	Selbstständige Tätigkeit
2007	Masterabschluss in Denkmalpflege und Umnutzung an der Berner Fachhochschule
2007–2010	Ressortleiterin Denkmalpflege und Kulturgüterschutz der Stadt Luzern
2010–	Kantonale Denkmalpflegerin

PETER OMACHEN (TEXTBEITRAG)

1964	Geboren in Luzern
1991	Architekturdiplom an der ETH Zürich
1991–2001	Mitarbeit in Luzerner Architekturbüros, MAS Geschichte und Theorie der Architektur an der ETH Zürich, Assistent an der ETH Zürich bei Prof. Werner Oechslin, Lehrstuhl für Architektur- und Kunstgeschichte, Redaktor der Architekturzeitschrift «archithese» sowie selbständige Tätigkeit als Architekturhistoriker und -journalist
2001–	Kantonaler Denkmalpfleger Obwalden Nebenamtlicher Dozent für Architekturgeschichte und Denkmalpflege an der Hochschule Luzern – Technik & Architektur
2009	Doktorat an der ETH Zürich, in Buchform erschienen: «Luzern – eine Touristenstadt. Hotelarchitektur 1782 bis 1914», Baden 2010
2013–	Mitglied der Eidgenössischen Kommission für Denkmalpflege EKD

IWAN BÜHLER

1958	Born in Lucerne
1987	Graduated in Architecture, ETH Zurich under Prof. Dolf Schnebli
1988–1989	Employed at the architectural office of Anton Bühlmann, Hergiswil
1990–1992	Assistant, ETH Zurich under Prof. André Corboz, Chair of Urban Planning
1990–	Own architectural office in Lucerne

CONY GRÜNENFELDER (ARTICLE)

1963	Born in Lucerne
1984	Completed apprenticeship as an interior draughtswoman
1993	Graduated in Architecture (HTL), Zentralschweizerisches Technikum Luzern
1993–2004	Employed at the architectural office Iwan Bühler, Lucerne
2004–2007	Freelance work
2007	Master in Conservation and Conversion at the Bern University of Applied Sciences
2007–2010	Head of Department of Monument Preservation and Cultural Heritage Conservation, City of Lucerne
2010–	Cantonal Monument Preservation Officer, Lucerne

PETER OMACHEN (ARTICLE)

1964	Born in Lucerne
1991	Graduate in Architecture, ETH Zurich
1991–2001	Employed at architectural offices in Lucerne, MAS in History and Theory of Architecture, ETH Zurich, Assistant, ETH Zurich under Prof. Werner Oechslin, Chair of History of Architecture and Art, editor of the architectural magazine *archithese*, freelance architectural historian and journalist
2001–	Cantonal Monument Preservation Officer Part-time Lecturer in History of Architecture and Monument Preservation, Lucerne School of Engineering and Architecture
2009	Doctorate, ETH Zurich, published thesis entitled: *Luzern – eine Touristenstadt. Hotelarchitektur 1782 bis 1914*, Baden 2010
2013–	Member of the Federal Commission for Monument Preservation (EKD)

DANKSAGUNG

Mein ausserordentlicher Dank gebührt an erster Stelle dem Bauherrn Yunfeng Gao, der mit seinen Mitarbeitern Chengbin Miao und Lijun Yu von Beginn an, fortwährend und bis zum Schluss grosses Vertrauen in unsere Ideen und unsere Arbeit gesetzt hat.

Nicht genügend Dank kann ich meinen Mitarbeiterinnen und Mitarbeitern aussprechen, die mit unermüdlichem Einsatz massgeblich zum Werdegang dieses einmaligen Projekts und zur Entstehung dieses Buches beigetragen haben. Nur dank ihrer hervorragenden Leistungen konnte das Erreichte erst gelingen.

Auch möchte ich Heinz Wirz und Antonia Chavez-Wirz sowie deren Team im Quart Verlag erwähnen und mich für die professionelle Begleitung und die äusserst angenehme Zusammenarbeit bedanken.

Ein besonderer Dank gilt den Sponsorenfirmen, deren finanzielle Unterstützungen wesentlich zum Entstehen dieses Buches beigetragen haben. Ihr kulturelles Engagement ermöglicht ein freundschaftliches und fruchtbares Zusammenwirken von Baukultur und Bauwirtschaft.

Zuletzt noch danke an alle Planerinnen und Planer, Unternehmerinnen und Unternehmer, Behördenvertreterinnen und Behördenvertreter und alle Unerwähnten, an jeden Einzelnen und jede Einzelne, ohne deren Beitrag das Hotel Palace nicht in der Form erstrahlen würde, wie es heute der Fall ist.

Im Januar 2023, Iwan Bühler

ACKNOWLEDGEMENTS

First of all, I am extremely grateful to the client Yunfeng Gao, who, together with his employees Chengbin Miao and Lijun Yu, have always shown such faith in our ideas and work from the beginning to the end of the project.

It is impossible to offer enough thanks to my employees, whose tireless efforts have had a decisive effect on the development of this unique project and the production of this book, which could never have been achieved without their exceptional support.

I also wish to thank Heinz Wirz, Antonia Chavez-Wirz and the team at Quart for their professional supervision and their extremely agreeable collaboration.

Special thanks to the sponsoring companies, whose financial support made a key contribution to the production of this volume. Their cultural engagement enables cordial, fruitful cooperation between building culture and the building sector.

Finally, many thanks to all the planners, contractors, authorities and all those who have not been mentioned, each and every one, without whom the Hotel Palace would not look so magnificent today.

Iwan Bühler, January 2023

FINANZIELLE UND IDEELLE UNTERSTÜTZUNG

Ein besonderer Dank gilt den Institutionen und Sponsorfirmen, deren finanzielle Unterstützungen wesentlich zum Entstehen dieses Buchs beigetragen haben. Ihr kulturelles Engagement ermöglicht ein fruchtbares und freundschaftliches Zusammenwirken von Baukultur und Bauwirtschaft.

FINANCIAL AND CONCEPTUAL SUPPORT

Special thanks to our sponsors and institutions whose financial support has helped us so much with the production of this book. Their cultural commitment is a valuable contribution to fruitful and cordial collaboration between the culture and economics of architecture.

Schweizerische Eidgenossenschaft
Confédération suisse
Confederazione Svizzera
Confederaziun svizra

Eidgenössisches Departement des Innern EDI
Bundesamt für Kultur BAK

Arnet & Co. AG, Emmenbrücke

Boschian Keramik AG, Kriens

Dreicon AG, Zürich

Durrer Technik AG, Adligenswil

Emilio Stecher AG, Root

First Swiss Hotel Collection AG

Gebr. Vogel & Co. AG, Malters

Halter & Colledani AG, Sarnen

Haupt AG, Ruswil

Herzog Haustechnik AG, Luzern

INVITA Hospitality Projects BAULINK AG, Chur

Itten+Brechbühl AG, Zürich

Jos. Berchtold AG, Zürich

Karl Bucher AG, Goldau

Kramis Teppich Design AG, Altbüron

Kurt Wohndesign AG, Obfelden

LICHTTEAM, Rothenburg / Luzern

Mandarin Oriental Palace Luzern

Marazzi Natursteine AG, Kreuzlingen

Maréchaux Elektro AG, Luzern

Marti Bauunternehmung AG, Luzern

MVM AG, Emmen

Molteni & C Spa, Giussano (Italien)

Neon Technik AG, Kemptthal

PZM Luzern AG, Horw

Schindler Aufzüge AG, Ebikon

Schüpfer und Debon Stuckwerk AG, Kriens

Simeta AG, Niederwil

SKK Landschaftsarchitekten AG, Wettingen

Tschopp Holzbau AG, Hochdorf

V-ZUG AG

W&P Engineering AG, Willisau

WAM Planer und Ingenieure AG, Bern

WBG AG – Visuelle Kommunikation, Zürich

IMPRESSUM

Hotel Palace Luzern
Denkmalpflegerische Erneuerung
Iwan Bühler Architekten

Herausgegeben von: Iwan Bühler, Luzern
Konzept: Heinz Wirz, Iwan Bühler, Luzern
Projektleitung: Quart Verlag, Antonia Chavez-Wirz

Textbeiträge: Peter Omachen, Luzern; Iwan Bühler, Luzern;
André Bachmann, Luzern; Birgit Roller, Luzern;
Sven Reithel, Wettingen; Silvan Birrer, Willisau;
Cony Grünenfelder, Luzern
Vorwort: Kuno Zimmermann und Franziska Willers, Zürich
Textlektorat deutsch: Eva Guttmann, Graz
Übersetzung deutsch – englisch: Benjamin Liebelt, Berlin

Grafisches Konzept: BKVK, Basel – Beat Keusch,
Ladina Ingold
Grafische Umsetzung: Quart Verlag Luzern
Lithos: Printeria, Luzern
Druck: DZA Druckerei zu Altenburg GmbH, Altenburg

Fotos / Bildrechte: Ruedi Walti, Basel; ausser: Archiv
Iwan Bühler Architekten, Luzern, S. 46 (oben), 47 (oben),
53 (rechts unten), 57, 87, 92 (rechts), 100 (unten), 109
(unten rechts), 110 (unten), 126, 127; Archiv Kantonale
Denkmalpflege, Luzern, S. 113; Baudokumentation von
ZSCHOKKE SCHÄFER BERN AG, 1994, S. 50–51, 52, 53
(links oben und unten); Dada – Heinz Dahinden Fotografie,
Luzern, S. 90, 91; Cony Grünenfelder, Luzern, S. 102; https://
www.historichotelsthenandnow.com/palacelucerne.html
(zuletzt abgerufen: 8.9.2022), S. 55 (oben); Privatarchiv
Jürg Reinshagen, Luzern, S. 60, 61; Birgit Roller, Luzern, S. 93
(links); Stadtarchiv Luzern: F2 PA 02/111:01, Fotograf:
unbekannt, S. 8/9; F2 PA 02/22:04, Fotograf:
Rudolf Schlatter, Zürich, S. 10/11; F2a/Strassen/Halden-
strasse 10.02:01, Fotograf: Rudolf Schlatter, Zürich, S. 12;
F2 PA 02/22:10, Fotograf: Rudolf Schlatter Zürich, S. 13;
F2 PA 02/22:11, Fotograf: unbekannt, S. 14, 92 (links); F2a/
Strassen/Haldenstrasse 10.02:02, Fotograf: Rudolf Schlatter,
Zürich, S. 15; F2 PA 02/22:08, Fotograf: Rudolf Schlatter,
Zürich, S. 16; F2a/Strassen/Haldenstrasse 10.02:03, Fotograf:
Rudolf Schlatter, Zürich, S. 17; F2 PA 02/22:09, Fotograf:
Rudolf Schlatter, Zürich, S. 18/19; F2 PA 02/22:07, Fotograf:
Rudolf Schlatter, Zürich, S. 20, 100 (oben); F2 PA 02/22:05,
Fotograf: Rudolf Schlatter, Zürich, S. 21; F2a/Strassen/
Haldenstrasse 10, S. 28 (Mitte); F2a/Strassen/Haldenstrasse
0, S. 27; F2a/Strassen/Haldenstrasse 0, S. 28 (oben); F2a/
Strassen/Haldenstrasse 10:03, Fotograf: R. Schlatter, Zürich,
S. 30 (oben); F2a/Strassen/Haldenstrasse 10:01, Fotograf: R.
Schlatter, Zürich, S. 30 (unten); F2a/Strassen/Haldenstrasse
10:02, Fotograf: R. Schlatter, Zürich, S. 32; F2a/Strassen/
Haldenstrasse 4a, S. 33; S. 34–43; F2a/Strassen/Halden-
strasse 10.01:10, Fotograf: unbekannt, S. 45; S. 46 (unten);
F2a/Strassen/Haldenstrasse 10.02, Fotograf: Josef Brun, S. 47
(unten); S. 52, 53, 54; F2a/Strassen/Haldenstrasse 10.02:04,
Fotograf: Rudolf Schlatter, Zürich, S. 56 (oben); S. 57 (oben);
S. 80; F2 PA 22/22:09, Fotograf: Rudolf Schlatter, Zürich,
S. 82; F2 PA 22/22:11, Fotograf: unbekannt, S. 92 (links); F2a/
Strassen/Haldenstrasse 10.01:05, Fotograf: E. Goetz,
Luzern, S. 95 (oben); F2a/Strassen/Haldenstrasse 10.01:07,
Fotograf: E. Goetz, Luzern, S. 95 (unten); S. 103 (unten);
S. 109 (unten links); F2 PA 22/22:04, Fotograf: Rudolf
Schlatter, Zürich, S. 115 (unten); https://twitter.com/
ICSEMIRAMIS/status/1455109338243207168/photo/2
(zuletzt abgerufen: 8.9.2022), S. 28 (unten); Liselotte
Wechsler, Luzern, S. 88, 89; ZHB Luzern Sondersammlung
S. 25, 44, 48, 49, 54 (oben), 56 (Mitte und unten)

IMPRINT

Hotel Palace Lucerne
Heritage Renovation
Iwan Bühler Architekten

Edited by: Iwan Bühler, Lucerne
Concept: Heinz Wirz, Iwan Bühler, Lucerne
Project management: Quart Verlag, Antonia Chavez-Wirz

Articles by: Peter Omachen, Lucerne; Iwan Bühler, Lucerne;
André Bachmann, Lucerne; Birgit Roller, Lucerne;
Sven Reithel, Wettingen; Silvan Birrer, Willisau;
Cony Grünenfelder, Lucerne
Foreword: Kuno Zimmermann and Franziska Willers, Zurich
German proofreading: Eva Guttmann, Graz
German – English translation: Benjamin Liebelt, Berlin

Graphic concept: BKVK, Basel – Beat Keusch, Ladina Ingold
Graphic design: Quart Verlag Luzern
Lithos: Printeria, Lucerne
Printing: DZA Druckerei zu Altenburg GmbH, Altenburg

Photos / Image rights: Ruedi Walti, Basel; except:
Archiv Iwan Bühler Architekten, Lucerne, p. 46 (top), 47 (top),
53 (right bottom), 57, 87, 92 (right), 100 (bottom), 109 (bottom
right), 110 (bottom), 126, 127; Cantonal Monument Authority
Archive, Lucerne, p. 113; building documentation by ZSCHOKKE
SCHÄFER BERN AG, 1994, p. 50–51, 52, 53 (left top and bottom);
Dada – Heinz Dahinden Fotografie, Lucerne, p. 90, 91; Cony
Grünenfelder, Lucerne, p. 102; https://www.historichotelsthenand-
now.com/palacelucerne.html (last accessed: 8.9.2022), p. 55 (top);
private archive, Jürg Reinshagen, Lucerne, p. 60, 61; Birgit Roller,
Lucerne, p. 93 (left); Lucerne City Archive: F2 PA 02/111:01,
photographer: unknown, p. 8/9; F2 PA 02/22:04, photographer:
Rudolf Schlatter, Zurich, p. 10/11; F2a/Strassen/Haldenstrasse
10.02:01, photographer: Rudolf Schlatter, Zurich, p. 12; F2 PA
02/22:10, photographer: Rudolf Schlatter Zurich, p. 13; F2 PA
02/22:11, photographer: unknown, p. 14, 92 (left); F2a/Strassen/
Haldenstrasse 10.02:02, photographer: Rudolf Schlatter, Zurich,
p. 15; F2 PA 02/22:08, photographer: Rudolf Schlatter, Zurich, p. 16;
F2a/Strassen/Haldenstrasse 10.02:03, photographer: Rudolf
Schlatter, Zurich, p. 17; F2 PA 02/22:09, photographer: Rudolf
Schlatter, Zurich, p. 18/19; F2 PA 02/22:07, photographer: Rudolf
Schlatter, Zurich, p. 20, 100 (top); F2 PA 02/22:05, photographer:
Rudolf Schlatter, Zurich, p. 21; F2a/Strassen/Haldenstrasse 10, p. 28
(centre); F2a/Strassen/Haldenstrasse 0, p. 27; F2a/Strassen/
Haldenstrasse 0, p. 28 (top); F2a/Strassen/Haldenstrasse 10:03,
photographer: R. Schlatter, Zurich, p. 30 (top); F2a/Strassen/
Haldenstrasse 10:01, photographer: R. Schlatter, Zurich, p. 30
(bottom); F2a/Strassen/Haldenstrasse 10:02, photographer:
R. Schlatter, Zurich, p. 32; F2a/Strassen/Haldenstrasse 4a, p. 33;
p. 34–43; F2a/Strassen/Haldenstrasse 10.01:10, photographer:
unknown, p. 45; p. 46 (bottom); F2a/Strassen/Haldenstrasse 10.02,
photographer: Josef Brun, p. 47 bottom; p. 52, 53, 54; F2a/Strassen/
Haldenstrasse 10.02:04, photographer: Rudolf Schlatter, Zurich,
p. 56 (top); p. 57 (top); p. 80; F2 PA 22/22:09, photographer: Rudolf
Schlatter, Zurich, p. 82; F2 PA 22/22:11, photographer: unknown,
p. 92 (left); F2a/Strassen/Haldenstrasse 10.01:05, photographer:
E. Goetz, Lucerne, p. 95 (top); F2a/Strassen/Haldenstrasse 10.01:07,
photographer: E. Goetz, Lucerne, p. 95 (bottom); p. 103 (bottom);
p. 109 (bottom left); F2 PA 22/22:04, photographer: Rudolf
Schlatter, Zurich, p. 115 (bottom); https://twitter.com/
ICSEMIRAMIS/status/1455109338243207168/photo/2 (last
accessed: 8.9.2022), p. 28 (bottom); Liselotte Wechsler, Lucerne,
p. 88, 89; Lucerne Central University Library, Special Collection,
p. 25, 44, 48, 49, 54 o., 56 (centre and bottom)